Eym 4'02

The Great Plains

MONTANA • NEBRASKA • NORTH DAKOTA SOUTH DAKOTA • WYOMING

By
Thomas G. Aylesworth
Virginia L. Aylesworth

CHELSEA HOUSE PUBLISHERS
New York • Philadelphia

First Printing

1   3   5   7   9   8   6   4   2

Library of Congress Cataloging-in-Publication Data

Aylesworth, Thomas G.
  The Great Plains: Montana, Nebraska, North Dakota, South Dakota,
Wyoming
Thomas G. Aylesworth, Virginia L. Aylesworth.
    p. cm.—(Discovering America)
  Includes bibliographical references and index.
  Summary: Discusses the geographical, historical, and cultural aspects of
Montana, North Dakota, and South Dakota, using maps, illustrated fact
spreads, and other illustrated material to highlight the land, history, and
people of each individual state.
    ISBN 0-7910-3404-6.
      0-7910-3422-4 (pbk.)
  1. West (U.S.)—Juvenile literature. 2. Montana—Juvenile literature. 3. North Dakota—Juvenile
literature. 4. South Dakota—Juvenile literature. [1. Great Plains. 2. Montana. 3. North Dakota.
4. South Dakota.] I. Aylesworth, Virginia L. II. Title. III. Series: Aylesworth, Thomas G. Discovering
America.

F597.A95 1996   94-45823
978—dc20   CIP
                                            AC

CONTENTS

Montana

The state seal of Montana, adopted in 1893, depicts a landscape. A plow, pick, and shovel, symbolizing agriculture and mining, are in the foreground. Mountains, trees, and the Great Falls of the Missouri River in the background represent the state's natural beauty and resources. A ribbon with the state motto appears at the bottom. The border is inscribed "The Great Seal of the State of Montana."

MONTANA

At a Glance

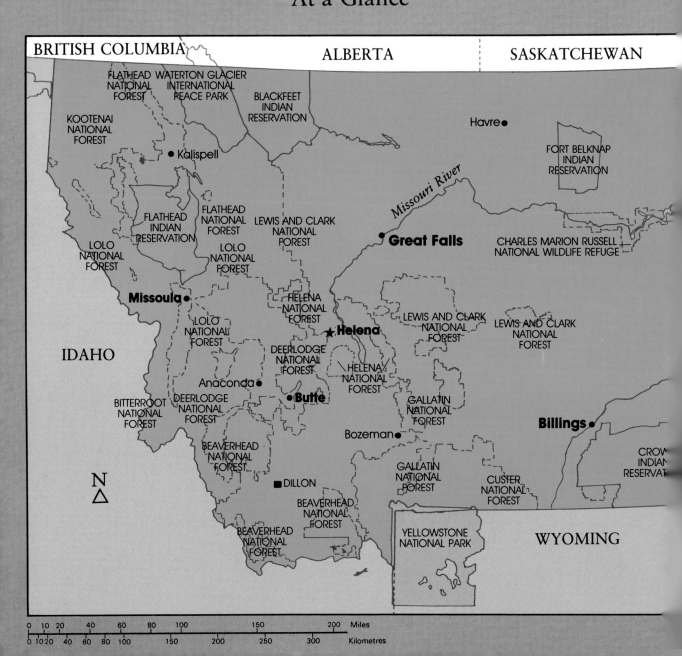

BRITISH COLUMBIA   ALBERTA   SASKATCHEWAN

FLATHEAD NATIONAL FOREST

WATERTON GLACIER INTERNATIONAL PEACE PARK

BLACKFEET INDIAN RESERVATION

KOOTENAI NATIONAL FOREST

Havre●

FORT BELKNAP INDIAN RESERVATION

● Kalispell

FLATHEAD INDIAN RESERVATION

FLATHEAD NATIONAL FOREST

LEWIS AND CLARK NATIONAL FOREST

Missouri River

LOLO NATIONAL FOREST

LOLO NATIONAL FOREST

● Great Falls

CHARLES MARION RUSSELL NATIONAL WILDLIFE REFUGE

IDAHO

Missoula●

LOLO NATIONAL FOREST

HELENA NATIONAL FOREST

★ Helena

LEWIS AND CLARK NATIONAL FOREST

LEWIS AND CLARK NATIONAL FOREST

DEERLODGE NATIONAL FOREST

HELENA NATIONAL FOREST

Anaconda●

DEERLODGE NATIONAL FOREST

● Butte

GALLATIN NATIONAL FOREST

BITTERROOT NATIONAL FOREST

Billings●

Bozeman●

BEAVERHEAD NATIONAL FOREST

CROW INDIAN RESERVAT

N
△

■ DILLON

GALLATIN NATIONAL FOREST

CUSTER NATIONAL FOREST

BEAVERHEAD NATIONAL FOREST

BEAVERHEAD NATIONAL FOREST

YELLOWSTONE NATIONAL PARK

WYOMING

| 0 | 10 | 20 | 40 | 60 | 80 | 100 | 150 | 200 | Miles |
| 0 | 10 20 | 40 | 60 | 80 | 100 | 150 | 200 | 250 | 300 | Kilometres |

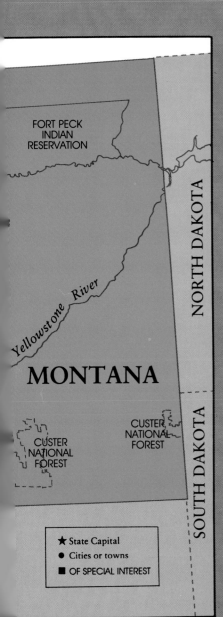

FORT PECK
INDIAN
RESERVATION

NORTH DAKOTA

Yellowstone River

MONTANA

CUSTER
NATIONAL
FOREST

CUSTER
NATIONAL
FOREST

SOUTH DAKOTA

★ State Capital
● Cities or towns
■ OF SPECIAL INTEREST

State Flag

Capital: Helena

Major Industries:
Lumber, mining, metallurgy,
petroleum, agriculture, livestock

Major Crops:
Grains, sugar beets, hay, flax

Size: 147,046 square miles (4th largest)
Population: 823,697 (44th largest)

State Bird:
Western Meadowlark

State Flag

The state flag, adopted in 1905, consists of the design from the state seal centered on a bright blue field, with gold fringe borders in the upper and lower edges.

State Motto

Oro y Plata

The Spanish motto, which means "gold and silver," refers to the state's mineral resources.

Glacier National Park, created by Congress in 1910, lies in the Northern Rockies.

State Capital
  Helena has been the capital of Montana since 1875, fourteen years before statehood.

State Name and Nickname
  The name Montana comes from the Spanish word *montaña*, meaning "mountain."
  Montana is known as the *Big Sky Country* because of its large area of rugged mountains and valleys.

State Flower
  Bitterroot, *Lewisia rediviva*, was named state flower in 1895, following a statewide vote conducted by the Montana Floral Emblem Association.

State Tree
  In 1949, the ponderosa pine, *Pinus ponderosa*, was designated state tree.

State Bird
  The western meadowlark, *Sturnella neglecta*, was adopted as state bird following a vote of schoolchildren.

State Animal
  The grizzly bear, *Ursus arctos horribilis*, was chosen state animal in 1983.

State Fish
  In 1977, the blackspotted cutthroat trout, *Salmo clarki*, was selected state fish.

State Gems
  The sapphire and Montana agate were named state gems in 1969.

State Grass
  Bluebunch grass, *Agropyron spicatum*, was designated state grass in 1973.

State Slogan
  The state slogan of Montana, "Naturally Inviting Montana," is used to promote tourism.

State Songs
  "Montana," with words by Charles C. Cohen and music by Joseph E. Howard, was chosen state song in 1945. In the same year, "Montana Melody," written by Carleen and LeGrande Harvey, was named official state ballad.

Population
  The population of Montana in 1992 was 823,697, making it the 44th most populous state. There are 5.43 people per square mile. Only three states have a larger area and only two states have a lower population density. About 24 percent of the people of Montana live in metropolitan areas, of which the Billings and Great Falls areas are the largest. Almost half of the state's population lives in agricultural areas. Approximately 98 percent of Montanans were born in the United States. Ancestors of today's Montanans were from Great Britain, Ireland, Germany, France, the Netherlands, the Scandinavian countries, and Poland.
  About 5 percent of Montana

residents are of Indian descent and approximately two-thirds of this population reside on reservations covering five million acres of land. The Blackfoot, Crow, Confederated Salish and Kootenai, Assiniboin, Gros Ventre, Sioux, Northern Cheyenne, Chippewa, and Cree tribes live on these reservations.

The majority of Montanans are Protestants, but the Roman Catholic community is the largest single religious group. Many Indians were nominally converted to Roman Catholicism by missionaries.

Industries

The principal industries of the state are agriculture, timber, mining, tourism, oil, and gas. The chief manufactured products are food products, wood and paper products, primary metals, printing and publishing, and petroleum and coal products.

Agriculture

The chief crops of the state are wheat, barley, sugar beets, hay, and oats. Montana is also a livestock state; there are estimated to be 2.6 million cattle, 225,000 hogs and pigs, 688,000 sheep, and 780,000 chickens and turkeys on its farms. Douglas fir, pines, and larch are harvested. Gold and copper are important mineral resources.

Government

The governor is elected to a four-year term, as are the lieutenant governor, attorney general, auditor, secretary of state, and superintendent of public instruction. The state legislature, which meets in odd-numbered years, consists of a 50-member senate and a 100-member house of representatives. Each of the 50 senatorial districts elects one senator to a four-year term, and each of the 100 representative districts elects one representative to a two-year term. The second and

most recent state constitution was adopted in 1973. In addition to its two United States senators, Montana has one representative in the U.S. House of Representatives. The state has three votes in the electoral college.

Sports

Many sporting events on the collegiate and secondary school levels are played throughout the state. Montana offers vast opportunities for almost every kind of outdoor sport. Summer recreational activities include boating, water skiing, biking, horseback riding, mountain climbing, and pack trips into wilderness areas. Montana's most popular winter sport is skiing.

Major Cities

Billings (population 81,125). Founded in 1882 by the Northern Pacific Railway, Montana's largest city lies on the west bank of the Yellowstone River. Named for the line's president, Frederick

Billings, earlier settlement had been prevented by hostile Indians until after the Sioux War of 1876. Gold and silver were discovered here in 1864. Today it is a major trade center for the region. Agriculture, tourism, and oil are the city's main industries.

Things to see in Billings:
Chief Black Otter Trail, Range Rider of the Yellowstone, Boothill Cemetery, Yellowstone Art Center, Peter Yegen Jr. Museum, Western Heritage Center, Indian Caves.

Great Falls (population 55,125). Originally surveyed in 1882 by Paris Gibson, this site was platted in 1884. The city is named after the Great Falls of the Missouri River, first reported by Meriwether Lewis and William Clark in 1805. The innovative planning of this city included 25 parks and playgrounds. It is the financial, commercial, and industrial center of this mining, agricultural, and stockraising center of northern Montana. Other industries include smelting; the refining of copper and zinc; and the manufacture of copper, aluminum wire, and cable.

Things to see in Great Falls:
Original art studio and museum of the western painter and sculptor Charles M. Russell.

Helena (population 24,609). Settled in 1864, the town was originally called Last Chance

Headstones mark the spots where George Custer and 210 of his men fell to the Sioux and Cheyenne on June 25, 1876.

Gulch after four discouraged prospectors explored the area as their "last chance" to find gold. Eventually the gulch and the area around it produced $20 million in gold. Renamed Helena, it was designated state capital in 1894. The silver boom ended in 1893, but during World War I, the demand for metals created mining activity in Helena. Agriculture, smelting, and ore refining are important to the city's economy, and it is a trading and transportation center for mining, livestock, and agricultural enterprises.

Things to see in Helena:
State Capitol, Montana Historical Society Museum, Original Governor's Mansion, Holter Museum of Art, Pioneer Cabin (1864), Gates of the Mountains, and Frontier Town.

Places to Visit

The National Park Service maintains seven areas in the state of Montana: Big Hole National Battlefield, Custer Battlefield National Monument, Glacier National

Montana is "Big Sky Country;" it houses wide plains in the east and tall, rugged mountains in the west.

Park, Fort Union Trading Post National Historic Site, Grant-Kohrs Ranch National Historic Site, three of the five entrances to Yellowstone National Park, and part of the Bighorn Canyon National Recreation Area. There are also 26 state recreation areas.

Chinook: Chief Joseph Battleground State Monument. This is the site of the last battle between the U.S. Army and the Nez Percé Indians.

Drummond: Bearmouth Ghost Town. Visitors are invited to search for a baking powder can containing a fortune, which is supposedly buried here.

Great Falls: Charles M. Russell Museum Complex and Original Studio. The museum features the work of cowboy artist Charles M. Russell.

Whitehall: Lewis and Clark Caverns State Park. The limestone cavern located in this 2,735-acre park contains intricate passageways and multicolored formations.

Events

There are many events and organizations that schedule activities of various kinds in the state of Montana. Here are some of them.

Sports: NRA/MRA Rodeo (Big Timber), College National Finals Rodeo (Bozeman), Montana Pro Rodeo Circuit Finals (Great Falls), Governor's Cup Sled Dog Races (Helena), Copper Cup Regatta (Polson), Great American Ski Chase (West Yellowstone), Wild Horse Stampede (Wolf Point).

Arts and Crafts: Festival of the Arts (Big Fork), Threshing Bee and Antique Show (Culbertson).

Music: Traditional Jazz Festival (Helena), Montana State Fiddlers' Contest (Polson), Music Festival (Red Lodge).

Entertainment: Montana Fair (Billings), Northern International Livestock Exposition Spring Show (Billings), Midland Empire Horse Show (Billings), Montana Winter Fair (Bozeman), Festival of Nations (Butte), Harvest Festival (Glasgow), Northeast Montana Fair and Rodeo (Glasgow), State Fair (Great Falls), Little Big Horn Days (Hardin), Crow Fair (Hardin), Havre Festival Days (Havre), Vigilante Parade (Helena), Governor's Cup All-Breeds Horse Show (Helena), Agriculture-Farm Show (Kalispell), Glacier International Horse Show (Kalispell), Libby Logger Days and River Races (Libby), Nordicfest (Libby), Park County Fair and O'Mok-See (Livingston), Milk River Wagon Train (Malta), Western Montana Quarter Horse Show (Missoula), Festival of Nations (Red Lodge), Opeta-Ye-Teca Indian Celebration (Wolf Point).

Tours: Yellowstone River Float Trip (Billings), Old No. 1 (Butte), Last Chancer Tour Train (Helena).

Theater: Bigfork Summer Playhouse (Bigfork), Montana Cowboy Poetry Gathering (Big Timber), Fort Peck Summer Theater (Glasgow), Old Opera House (Virginia City), Playmill Theater (West Yellowstone).

The Missouri River originates in Montana at the junction of the Gallatin, Jefferson, and Madison Rivers. From here it flows north and then east to irrigate much of northern Montana. The Missouri is the country's second longest river and a major artery of trade and commerce.

The Bighorn Canyon National Recreation Area is located in the southernmost part of the state, near Montana's border with Wyoming.

The Land and the Climate

Montana is bounded on the west and southwest by Idaho, on the southeast by Wyoming, on the east by North and South Dakota, and on the north by the Canadian provinces of British Columbia, Alberta, and Saskatchewan. There are two major land regions in the state: the Great Plains and the Rocky Mountains.

The Great Plains make up the eastern three-fifths of Montana. This gently rolling highland is part of the vast Interior Plain of North America, which stretches from Canada to Mexico. The land here is ideal for grain crops and for sheep and cattle ranching. There are also oil wells in the region. The terrain is varied by hills and wide river valleys, with occasional mountains.

The Rocky Mountains cover western Montana, forming a landscape of striking beauty. Grassy valleys and towering mountains, evergreen forests and sparkling lakes make up the scenery. On the highest peaks is perpetual snow, and there are a few active glaciers and many permanent snow fields. The most important of the more than 50 mountain ranges in the region are the Absaroka, Beartooth, Beaverhead, Big Belt, Bitterroot, Bridger, Cabinet, Flathead, Gallatin, Little Belt, Madison, Mission, Swan, and Tobacco Root. It is a region of forest products and asbestos, gold, zinc, manganese, silver, lead, and copper mines.

Three important river systems drain the state: the Missouri, including its Yellowstone branch; the Columbia; and the Nelson-Saskatchewan systems. Montana has only one large natural lake—Flathead Lake in the northwest, which covers about 189 square miles. But there are numerous smaller lakes, including 250 in Glacier National Park alone.

Montana's weather varies markedly from east to west. Temperatures west of the Continental Divide (the land elevation that separates waters running west to the Pacific Ocean from those running east to the Atlantic) are warmer in winter and cooler in summer than those in the east. Temperatures average 12 to 31 degrees Fahrenheit in January and 54 to 84 degrees F. in July. Snowfall is heavy in all parts of the state, with over 30 inches per year in the northwest—and 300 inches is not unheard of. An unusual climatic feature of Montana is the *chinook*—warm dry wind blowing down the eastern slopes of the mountains—which enables farmers to graze cattle on the ranges for short periods during the winter.

Below left:
The bison was once a common sight on the great plains of Montana. Today, it is almost extinct, along with the endangered kit fox, gray wolf, fisher, and Audubon sheep. Montana remains one of the nation's safest habitats for such animals as the buffalo, beaver, grizzly and black bear, moose, elk, coyote, and mountain lion.

Below:
The Pintler Scenic Route in the southwestern part of the state meanders through high mountain passes and along the shores of Georgetown Lake.

Western Montana is dominated by the breathtaking natural splendor of the Rocky Mountains and more than 50 mountain ranges. Visitors travel from all over to marvel at the striking scenery of such areas as Glacier National Park and to enjoy such sports as skiing and mountain climbing.

Above:
The great explorers Lewis and Clark first entered Montana in April 1805, traveling west on the Missouri River from the mouth of the Yellowstone.

Below:
A Crow Indian painting of a buffalo hunter. The Crow and other tribes such as the Cheyenne, Shoshone, Sioux, Mandan, and Nez Percé were encountered in the Montana region by 18th-century explorers.

The History

There were two groups of Indian tribes living in what is now Montana before the white man came. On the eastern plains were the Arapaho, the Assiniboin, the Blackfoot, the Cheyenne, and the Crow. In the western mountains were the Bannock, the Kalispel, the Kutenai, and the Shoshone. Other Great Plains Indians, including the Sioux, the Mandan, and the Nez Percé, came into the region to hunt buffalo and other game.

The French traders Pierre and François de la Vérendrye visited what is now Montana in 1743, but the area was largely unexplored and unknown until most of it was acquired by the United States as part of the Louisiana Purchase from France in 1803. Meriwether Lewis and William Clark led their party of explorers through the Montana region in 1805, opening a trail to the Pacific Ocean. They discovered what would be a famous landmark for later pioneers: 200-foot Pompey's Pillar, a gigantic rock rising above the Yellowstone River.

Two years later, in 1807, the establishment of Manuel Lisa's trading post at the mouth of the Big Horn River ushered in a half century of hunting and trapping. In 1847 the American Fur Company built the first permanent settlement in Montana at Fort Benton on the Missouri River. Then, in 1862, gold was discovered in Grasshopper Creek in southwestern Montana. When other strikes followed, the region was stampeded by gold seekers, with picturesque and lawless frontier towns springing up as fast as miners could build them: Virginia City, Bannack, Diamond City, and others. Until this time, Montana had been part of the Idaho Territory, but the high crime rate in the mining camps and towns necessitated closer governing, so the Montana Territory was created by the federal government in 1864.

Above:
General George Armstrong Custer, who led the U.S. 7th Cavalry at the Battle of Little Bighorn.

At left:
A U.S. military campaign was launched against the Sioux and Cheyenne Indians in 1876 to counter the growing threat of tribes angered by the careless slaughter of buffalo by white settlers and by U.S. violations of treaties. The Battle of Little Bighorn on June 25, 1876, seen here, was one of the Indians' last but greatest victories over the white man. More than 200 men of the U.S. 7th Cavalry, led by General George Armstrong Custer, met overwhelming numbers of Sioux and Cheyenne, led by Crazy Horse and Sitting Bull, along the Little Bighorn River, and Custer's entire command was annihilated. The battle is frequently referred to as "Custer's Last Stand."

Cattle ranching became important after the first longhorn herd was brought up from Texas in 1866 by a cattleman named Nelson Story. These thousand head of cattle gave a strong impetus to the ranching industry already established in the mountain valleys, and extension of the railroads into Montana made cattle raising even more profitable. But the extremely cold winter of 1886–87 killed thousands of animals and reduced the industry considerably.

Throughout this period the Indians were being pushed farther and farther west, off land that had been their own. Two of the most notorious Indian campaigns in American history were fought in the Montana Territory. On June 25, 1876, Custer's Last Stand was made near the Little Bighorn River in southern Montana. Part of the U.S.

Chief Joseph, known to his people as Hinmaton-Yalakit, led the Nez Percé Indians in their attempted flight to Canada to avoid eviction from their Wallowa Valley homeland to Idaho reservations. At Bear Paw Mountain in Montana, after a 1,000-mile retreat marked by 13 engagements with U.S. troops, Joseph and his followers were forced to surrender in 1877 and to give up all rights to their native territories.

7th Cavalry, led by the reckless general George A. Custer, was wiped out by Sioux and Cheyenne warriors under Crazy Horse, Gall, and Two Moons. The second action was the two-day battle at Big Hole in southwestern Montana in 1877. Chief Joseph of the Oregon Nez Percé was trying to lead his tribe through the territory to safety in Canada to avoid resettlement on a reservation. The thousand-mile flight of the Nez Percé ended at Big Hole with surrender to federal troops led by Colonel Nelson A. Miles.

Montana became the 41st state in 1889, after its population had risen to some 140,000. During the 1880s and 1890s silver was discovered in the rock ledges of Butte Hill. Then rich veins of copper were unearthed nearby. Smelters were built to refine the ore, and Butte Hill became known as "the Richest Hill on Earth."

During the early 1900s, Montana began to make increasing use of its rich natural resources. Dams were built, the railroads were extended, and new plants refined sugar, milled flour, and processed meat. The magnificent Glacier National Park was created in 1910. On the political side, Jeannette Rankin of Missoula was elected to the United States House of Representatives in 1916—several years before suffrage was granted to women on a national level.

During the Great Depression of the 1930s, Montana suffered primarily from the lack of demand for its metals. But the economy boomed again during World War II, when metals, grains, and meat were needed in great quantities for the war effort. Oil and natural gas production began in Great Plains, Montana, in 1915, expanded greatly in the 1950s, and peaked in the 1960s. Coal mining, which began with coal stoves and steam locomotives, increased dramatically in the 1970s.

The closing of the copper mines at Butte, the smelter in Anaconda, and the copper refinery at Great Falls in the early 1980s marked the end of the copper century and forced Montana's economy to evolve. A change in economic structure led Montana away from agriculture, forestry, and mining to concentrate on tourism and new, innovative businesses that provide jobs without contribut-

Far left:
American Indians are inseparable from Montana's cultural heritage. The Indian population, which has increased steadily since the 1950s, now constitutes the most significant ethnic minority in the state.

At left:
Screen legend Gary Cooper, born in Helena, was a cowboy before he went to Hollywood. Known for his low-key acting style, Cooper won Academy Awards for his roles in the films *Sergeant York* and *High Noon.*

ng to the deterioration of the state's natural resources and beauty. n recent years the state has become popular with vacationers because of its breathtaking natural beauty and outdoor recreational activities.

Education

Montana's first schools were started in the mining camps of the 860s, but they were privately owned and charged tuition. It was not until 1893 that the state guaranteed free public education. The first nstitution of higher education in Montana was Rocky Mountain College (1883). Ten years later, colleges and universities increased dramatically. Founded in 1893 were the University of Montana, Montana College of Mineral Science and Technology, Montana State University, and Western Montana College.

Famous People

Many famous people were born in or relocated to the state of Montana. Here are a few:

Dirk Benedict b. 1945, Helena. Television actor: *Battlestar Galactica, The A-Team*

William Andrews Clark 1839-1925, Pennsylvania. Businessman; U.S. senator

Gary Cooper 1901-61, Helena. Two-time Academy Award-winning film actor: *Sergeant York, High Noon*

Marcus Daly 1841-1900, Ireland. Businessman; politician; founder of Anaconda Copper Mining Co.

Patrick Duffy b. 1949, Townsend. Television actor: *Dallas*

Paris Gibson 1830-1920, Maine. Politician, promoter, and financier

A. B. Guthrie, Jr. 1901-91, Indiana. Pulitzer prize–winning author and journalist: *The Big Sky; The Way West*

Samuel Thomas Hauser 1833-1914, Kentucky. Pioneer financier; first resident governor of the Montana Territory

Chet Huntley 1911-74, Cardwell. Radio and television journalist

Phil Jackson b. 1945, Deer Lodge. Basketball player; coach for the Chicago Bulls

Myrna Loy 1905-93, Helena. Film actress: *The Thin Man; The Best Years of Our Lives*

David Lynch b. 1946, Missoula. Television and film director: *Twin Peaks, The Elephant Man*

Michael J. Mansfield b. 1903, New York. Educator and political leader

Jeannette Rankin 1880-1973, near Missoula. Suffragist and first woman member of Congress

Charles Marion Russell 1864-1926, Missouri. Cowboy, artist, and author who re-

Sacagawea 1787?-1812?, Western Montana or Idaho. Indian guide for the Lewis & Clark expedition

Thomas J. Walsh 1859-1933, Wisconsin. Political leader

Colleges and Universities

There are many colleges and universities in Montana. Here are the more prominent, with their locations, dates of founding, and undergraduate enrollments.

Eastern Montana College, Billings, 1927, 3,761

Montana College of Mineral Science and Technology, Butte, 1893, 1,975

Montana State University, Bozeman, 1893, 10,540

Rocky Mountain College, Billings, 1883, 769

University of Montana, Missoula, 1893, 10,614

Western Montana College, Dillon, 1897, 727

Where To Get More Information

Montana Travel Promotion Division
Department of Commerce
2030 11th Ave., P.O. Box 1730
Helena, MT 59624
or call, 1-800-541-1447

Nebraska

Pictured in the center of the state seal is a blacksmith at work, representing the mechanical arts; a settlers' cabin, stacks of corn, and sheaves of wheat, symbolizing agriculture; and a steamboat and train, representing transportation. The Rocky Mountains can be seen in the distance, and a ribbon containing the state motto floats above them. The border around the seal reads "Great Seal of the State of Nebraska" and "March 1st, 1867"—the date of the state's admission to the Union.

NEBRASKA
At a Glance

Capital: Lincoln

State Flag

Major Industries: Agriculture, livestock, food processing, machinery, electronics

Major Crops: Corn, sorghum, wheat, soybeans

State Flower:
Goldenrod

Size: 77,355 square miles (15th largest)
Population: 1,605,603 (36th largest)

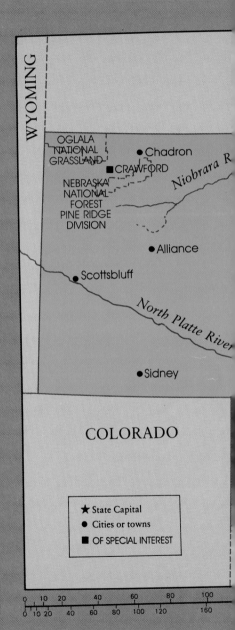

WYOMING

OGLALA
NATIONAL
GRASSLAND
● Chadron
■ CRAWFORD
NEBRASKA
NATIONAL
FOREST
PINE RIDGE
DIVISION
Niobrara R.

● Alliance

● Scottsbluff

North Platte River

● Sidney

COLORADO

★ State Capital
● Cities or towns
■ OF SPECIAL INTEREST

0 10 20   40   60   80   100
0 10 20   40   60   80   100 120   160

SOUTH DAKOTA

IOWA

NEBRASKA
NATIONAL
FOREST
NIOBRARA
DIVISION

SANTEE
INDIAN
RESERVATION

Elkhorn River

South Sioux City ●

WINNEBAGO
INDIAN
RESERVATION

North Loup River

NEBRASKA
NATIONAL
FOREST
BESSEY
DIVISION

Middle Loup River

Norfolk ●

NEBRASKA

OMAHA
INDIAN
RESERVATION

Missouri River

● North Platte

Columbus ●

Fremont ●

Omaha ●
Bellevue ●

Plattsmouth ●

Grand Island ●

● York

★ **Lincoln**

Lexington ●

Kearney ●

Nebraska City ●

Platte River

● Hastings

Holdrege ●

● Beatrice

● McCook

Fairbury ●

Falls City ●

MISSOURI

KANSAS

N
△

State Flag
The state flag, which was adopted in 1963, consists of the state seal printed in gold and silver on a dark blue field.

State Motto
Equality Before the Law
This motto, adopted in 1867, refers to one of the basic principles of the American system of justice.

A hay field stretches under the blue Nebraska sky.

State Capital
   Lincoln has been the capital since 1867, the year Nebraska became a state.

State Name and Nicknames
   The name Nebraska comes from the Omaha Indian word *Nebrathka*, meaning "flat water." It referred to the Platte River.
   The *Cornhusker State*, Nebraska's official nickname since 1945, refers to the method of harvesting, or "husking," corn. It was changed from the *Tree Planters' State*, which had been adopted in 1895. Unofficial nicknames include the *Antelope State* for its many herds of antelope, and the *Bug-Eating State* for its many bug-eating bull bats.

State Flower
   Goldenrod, *Solidago serotina*, was selected as state flower in 1895.

State Tree
   In 1972, the cottonwood, *Populus deltoides*, was adopted as state tree.

State Bird
   The western meadowlark, *Sturnella neglecta*, was named state bird in 1929.

State Day
   March 1 was designated state day in 1931.

State Fossil
   The mammoth was selected state fossil in 1967.

State Insect
   The honeybee, *apis mellifera*, was chosen state insect in 1975.

State Gemstone
   Blue agate was designated state gemstone in 1967.

State Grass
   Little bluestem was named official state grass in 1969.

State Mammal
   In 1981, the white-tailed deer, *Cariacus virginianus*, was selected state mammal.

State Rock
   Prairie agate was named state rock in 1967.

State Soil
   The state soil of Nebraska is typic arguistolls.

State Slogan
   "Welcome to Nebraskaland, where the West begins," was designated state slogan in 1963.

State Song
   "Beautiful Nebraska," with music by Jim Fras and words by Jim Fras and Guy G. Miller, was adopted as state song in 1967.

Population
   The population of Nebraska in 1992 was 1,605,603, making it the 36th most populous state. There are 20.4 people per square mile.

Industries
   The principal industries of the state are agriculture and food processing. The chief manufactured products are foods, machinery, electric and electronic equipment, primary and fabricated metal products, and transportation equipment.

Agriculture

The chief crops of the state are corn, sorghum, soybeans, hay, wheat, beans, oats, potatoes, and sugar beets. Nebraska is also a livestock state; there are estimated to be 6 million cattle, 4.2 million hogs and pigs, 160,000 sheep, 8.3 million chickens and turkeys on its farms. Portland cement, crushed stone, and construction sand and gravel are important mineral resources.

Government

The governor is elected to a four-year term, as are the secretary of state, attorney general, treasurer, and auditor. Nebraska is the only state whose legislature consists of one house. Its 49 members, called senators, are elected from 49 legislative districts and serve four-year terms. This unicameral legislature meets annually. The most recent state constitution was adopted in 1875. In addition to its two United States senators, Nebraska has three representatives in the U. S. House of Representatives. The state has five votes in the electoral college.

Sports

Many sporting events on the collegiate and secondary school levels are played throughout the state. In football, the University of Nebraska is a perennial power, having won the Orange Bowl in 1964, 1971, 1972, 1973, and 1983; the Sugar Bowl in 1974, 1985, and 1987; and the Cotton Bowl in 1974.

Although the state does not have any professional teams in the major sports leagues, the Omaha Racers are members of the Continental Basketball Association, which is the official developmental league of the National Basketball Association.

Major Cities

Lincoln (population 191,972). When Lincoln was named state capital in 1867, only thirty people lived in the town. By the mid-1870s, the population had grown to 2,500, and public utilities, a capitol building, a railroad line, and a university had been built. Today, Lincoln is the state's second largest city, as well as a major grain market and center for manufacturing, finance, and trade.

Things to see in Lincoln:
State Capitol, Lincoln Monument, Executive Mansion, University of Nebraska State Museum, Encounter Center, Lentz Center for Asian Culture, Ralph Mueller Planetarium, Sheldon Memorial Art Gallery and Sculpture Garden, Christlieb Collection of Western Art, Elder Art Gallery, Museum of Nebraska History, William Jennings Bryan Home (1902), Statehood Memorial—Thomas P. Kennard House (1869), Ferguson Mansion (1910), National Museum of Roller Skating, Folsom Children's Zoo, and Robber's Cave.

Omaha (population 335,719). Nebraska's largest city was founded in 1854, after the Omaha Indians signed a treaty with the federal government and left the area. The city soon became a supply center for wagon trains and prospectors headed west. Today, in addition to being home to the headquarters of the Strategic Air Command, Omaha is one of the largest livestock markets and meat-packing centers of the world.

Things to see in Omaha:
Joslyn Art Museum, Great Plains Black Museum, Omaha Children's Museum, Union Pacific Historical Museum, Old Market, Mutual of Omaha Dome, Henry Doorly Zoo, Western Heritage Museum/Omaha History Museum, Gerald Ford Birth Site, Mormon Pioneer Cemetery, Ak-Sar-Ben Field and Coliseum, Boys Town, Historic Bellevue, Strategic Air Command Museum, Fontenelle Forest, USS *Hazard*, USS *Marlin*, and St. Cecilia's Cathedral.

Places to Visit

The National Park Service maintains four areas in the state of Nebraska: Scotts Bluff National Monument, Homestead National Monument of America, Agate Fossil Beds National Monument, and Chimney Rock National Historic Site. In addition, there are 57 state recreation areas.

Auburn: Brownville. Visitors may tour restored buildings, including Dr. Spurgin's Dental Office and the Brownville Depot, in this riverboat town of the 1800s.
Chadron: Museum of the Fur Trade. Displays featuring frontier weapons, tanning equipment, and furs, trace the history of the nineteenth-century fur trade on the Missouri River.
Gothenburg: Pony Express Station. Originally located on the Oregon Trail, this building was used by the Pony Express from 1860 to 1861.
Hastings: Hastings Museum. Exhibits in this museum include mineral displays, Indian items, and pioneer artifacts.
Minden: Harold Warp Pioneer Village. This 26-building complex features an 1869 Indian fort, a pony express station, a general store, and a sod house.
Nebraska City: John Brown's Cave. This major stop of the Underground Railway was run by the great abolitionist.
North Platte: Buffalo Bill Ranch State Historical Park. This ranch, which includes an 18-room house and a barn, was the home of William F. Cody.
Red Cloud: Willa Cather Historical Center. Visitors may tour the childhood home of the author, and view exhibits on her life.

Events

There are many events and organizations that schedule activities of various kinds in the state of Nebraska. Here are some of them.
Sports: Little Britches State Rodeo (Chadron), horse racing at Agricultural Park (Columbus), Johnson Lake Yacht Club Annual Regatta (Lexington), Sailing Regatta (McCook), Buffalo Bill Rodeo (North Platte), Ogallala Round-up Rodeo (Ogallala), Governor's Cup Sailing Regatta (Ogallala), NCAA College Baseball World Series (Omaha), World's Championship Rodeo (Omaha), Old West Balloon Rally (Scottsbluff), Missouri River Raft

Regatta (South Sioux City), horse racing at Atokad Park (South Sioux City).

Arts and Crafts: Art in the Park Arts Festival (Kearney), Antique and Crafts Extravaganza (Lexington), Lincoln Gem and Mineral Club Show (Lincoln), Arbor Day Arts Festival (Nebraska City), Spring Festival of Crafts (Norfolk), Omaha Summer Arts Festival (Omaha), Orchid Show and Sale (Omaha).

Music: Flatwater Festival (Lincoln), Lincoln Symphony Orchestra (Lincoln), Nebraska Chamber Orchestra (Lincoln), Omaha Ballet (Omaha), Omaha Symphony (Omaha), Nebraska Choral Arts Society (Omaha), Nebraska State Country Music Championship (Springfield).

Entertainment: Homestead Days (Beatrice), "Gateway to the West" Days (Blair), Fur Trade Days (Chadron), Buckskin Rendezvous (Chadron), Lewis and Clark Tri-State Dairy Expo (Crofton), Northeast Nebraska Cow Chip Flip (Crofton), Crystal Springs Camp-in (Fairbury), Old Settlers Celebration and Parade (Fremont), John C. Frémont Days (Fremont), Oregon Trail Days (Gering), Pony Express Harvest Festival (Gothenburg), Nebraska Antique Airplane Association Fly-in (Gothenburg), Husker Harvest Days (Grand Island), Harvest of Harmony Festival and Parade (Grand Island), Swedish Days (Holdredge), Old Fashioned Fourth of July (Lexington), Camp Creek Antique Machinery and Threshing Association Festival (Lincoln), National Czech Festival (Lincoln), Nebraska State Fair (Lincoln), LaVitsef Celebration (Norfolk), Nebraskaland Days Celebration (North Platte), Indian Summer Rendezvous (Ogallala), River City Round-up (Omaha), Christmas at Union Station (Omaha), Fort Sidney Days and Rod 'n Roll (Sidney), Chicken Show (Wayne).

Tours: Oregon Trail Wagon Train (Bayard), *The Spirit of Brownville* cruises (Brownville), Tour of the Frank House (Kearney).

Theaters: Village Theater (Auburn), Post Playhouse (Crawford), Lincoln Community Playhouse (Lincoln), Christmas Pageant and Lights (Minden), Omaha Community Playhouse (Omaha), Orpheum Theater (Omaha), Emmy Gifford Children's Theater (Omaha).

Nebraska celebrates part of its immigrant history every year at the National Czech Festival in Lincoln.

The frontier trails of Nebraska were vital thorough-fares for westward-bound settlers and fur traders in the 19th century. The 1862 Homestead Act encouraged many travelers to settle in Nebraska and develop the farmland, although the state had once been known as the "Great American Desert" for its semi-arid prairies.

The Land and the Climate

Above:
The waters of the entire state drain into the Missouri River, which forms the eastern border of Nebraska. With almost 11,000 miles of rivers and streams, Nebraska counts water as one of its greatest natural resources. Much of this water supply comes from rain, snow, underground springs, and a huge runoff from the Rocky Mountains of Colorado, Montana, and Wyoming.

Above right:
Nebraska's sandhills area is characterized by grassy hills, small basins, wet and dry valleys, marshes, and lakes. Its sandy soil is typical of much of the state's land.

Nebraska is bounded on the west by Wyoming and Colorado, on the north by South Dakota, on the east by Iowa and Missouri, and on the south by Kansas and Colorado. The state has two major land areas, the Dissected Till Plains and the Great Plains.

The Dissected Till Plains are a section of glacier-formed lowlands in the eastern fifth of the state. It is an area of rich, hilly farmland, with vast fields of corn, oats, hay, wheat, rye, sorghum, and soybeans. Hogs, poultry, dairy cattle, and beef cattle are also raised.

The Great Plains cover the rest of the state, a region of flowing streams, abundant well water, and excellent grasses—ideal for cattle ranching. Crops of wheat, potatoes, barley, and hay are also found here. Some oil and natural-gas wells have been sunk in the region.

The principal rivers in Nebraska are the Missouri, which forms the eastern and northeastern border of the state, and the Platte, which is formed by the junction of the North and South Platte Rivers near the city of North Platte. The state has some 2,000 lakes, none of them very large.

Quick changes in temperature are not unusual in Nebraska, and are often responsible for the violent thunderstorms, hailstorms, tornadoes, and blizzards that hit the state. Hot breezes from the Gulf of Mexico can make summer weather uncomfortable in eastern Nebraska. In July, temperatures average 78 degrees Fahrenheit, and in January, 22 degrees F., with rainfall ranging between 18 and 27 inches yearly (higher in the east).

The History

The discovery of ancient tips for stone tools and weapons indicates that there were prehistoric Indians living in what was to become Nebraska between 10,000 and 25,000 years ago. When the first white men arrived in the territory, they found several Indian tribes. Some were peaceful farmers and hunters who lived along the rivers: tribes like the Missouri, the Omaha, the Oto, and the Ponea. The Pawnee were hunters and farmers, too, but they were fierce warriors who fought with the Sioux, who lived farther north. The Pawnee became friendly with the incoming white settlers, and Pawnee scouts would help the United States Army in wars against the Sioux during the 1800s.

To the west were the Arapaho, the Cheyenne, the Comanche, and the Sioux, hunting tribes who did not farm and dwelled in temporary villages. As white settlers drove other tribes from their land on the east, several tribes migrated into the Nebraska region. Among them were the Fox, the Iowa, and the Sauk in the 1830s, and the Santee Sioux in 1863. The last to settle were the Winnebago, who were driven from Wisconsin to Iowa, then to Minnesota, then to South Dakota; they finally arrived in Nebraska in 1863 and 1864.

Francisco Vásquez de Coronado, the Spanish explorer, led an expedition into mid-America in 1541, coming up from the southwest as far as Kansas. He claimed all this territory (including present-day Nebraska) for Spain, but the Spanish government made no settlements. In 1682 the French explorer Robert Cavelier (called La Salle) traveled down the Mississippi River and claimed all the land drained by the river for France, naming this huge expanse Louisiana. French traders and fur trappers moved in during the 1690s and early 1700s, and in 1714 Étienne Veniard de Bourgmont traveled up the Missouri River to the mouth of the Platte. Spain still felt that it controlled the region, and objected to the French invasion. In 1720 a

The famous Pony Express, which ran in part through southern Nebraska, was a mail-delivery service operated by rugged young horsemen who carried packages and letters from St. Joseph, Missouri, to Sacramento, California. Each rider changed horses every 10 miles and covered a distance of some 75 miles before being relieved by another, who seized the mail pouch and dashed off to continue the journey. Armed with knives and pistols, these daring young men rode day and night through hostile Indian country and covered almost 2,000 miles in 8 to 10 days.

Spanish expedition led by Pedro de Villasur marched from Santa Fe (now in New Mexico) to Nebraska, where they were defeated by a group of Pawnee Indians and forced to retreat.

Perhaps the first white men to cross the Nebraska region were Pierre and Paul Mallet, French explorers, in 1739. France gave the Louisiana Territory to Spain in 1762, but French trappers and fur traders continued to operate in the Nebraska region, and the Spaniards never could set up a proper government in the vast wilderness. In 1800 the ruler of France, Napoleon Bonaparte, forced Spain to return Louisiana, and three years later he sold the territory to the United States.

President Thomas Jefferson sent Meriwether Lewis and William Clark on their famous expedition of 1804–06, and they explored the eastern edge of Nebraska. Another American explorer, Zebulon M. Pike, traversed the south-central part of the territory in 1806. A Spanish-American trader named Manuel Lisa set up fur-trading posts along the Missouri River between 1807 and 1820, and the Oregon Trail was opened by fur agent Robert Stuart en route from the Astoria fur-trading post in Oregon to New York City. But because of its semi-arid prairies, travelers through Nebraska considered it unfit for farming—they called it "the Great American Desert."

In 1823 the U.S. Army established Fort Atkinson on the Missouri River, about 16 miles north of present-day Omaha. The fort was th ite of Nebraska's first school, library, sawmill, gristmill, and rickyard. In 1823 the first permanent settlement was established at ellevue, near Omaha.

The Kansas-Nebraska Act of 1854 created the Kansas and Nebraska Territories, and the Nebraska Territory included not only resent-day Nebraska, but also most of Montana, North Dakota, outh Dakota, Wyoming, and Colorado. According to local legend, ne border between the Kansas and Nebraska Territories was etermined by Febold Feboldson, "the Paul Bunyan of the Great lains," who wanted an absolutely straight border. As legend has it, e bred bees with eagles for 15 years, until he had an eagle-sized bee. Ie then hitched it to a plow and made a "beeline" between the two erritories.

Early settlers, called "sodbusters," built sod houses and attempted o conquer the prairies. The 1862 Homestead Act, giving 160 acres f western frontier country to every settler, brought a rush of omesteaders. In 1865 the Union Pacific Railroad began laying track

Above:
William Jennings Bryan, one of the nation's greatest political orators, came to Nebraska in 1887 as a practicing lawyer. After serving as a representative to Congress (1891–95), Bryan ran unsuccessfully for a seat in the Senate. He later became editor-in-chief of the Omaha *World Herald.* In 1896 Democratic Party members who favored currency based on silver rather than gold planned to nominate Bryan for the presidency. At the party's convention that year, Bryan delivered what is commonly acknowledged as the most impressive speech ever heard at a national convention. The enthusiasm he generated was such that Bryan won the nomination, but he lost the election to William McKinley. After two more unsuccessful tries for the presidency, Bryan was appointed Secretary of State under Woodrow Wilson and was influential as an advocate for farmers and laborers and a supporter of Wilson's social-reform measures.

t right:
Villiam Frederick Cody, etter known as "Buffalo ill," was perhaps the West's nost renowned scout, hunter, nd showman. He began his reat "Wild West" exhibition ear North Platte, Nebraska, 1883. The show, which oured throughout the ountry, glorified Buffalo Bill's xploits with the Indians and is prowess as a buffalo unter.

COL. W. F. CODY

I AM COMING

Father Edward Joseph Flanagan founded the Boys Town orphanage for underprivileged youngsters near Omaha, Nebraska. After winning national recognition for fostering leadership in his boys, he was sent by the U.S. government to Europe and the Far East after World War II to help establish orphanages for the needy abroad.

westward from Omaha, and in 1867 Nebraska became the 37th state in the Union.

After a brief setback in the 1870s, when grasshoppers ruined the crops, a second wave of settlers began to arrive. Demand for land raised prices and credit purchases became common, until drought collapsed the market in the 1890s. Irrigation, cooperatives, and conservative farming methods helped strengthen the economy after 1900, and Nebraska began to prosper. Where crops could not be grown, cattle were raised.

Nebraska was extremely hard hit by the Great Depression of the 1930s. Farm prices fell, as they did everywhere, but Nebraska was also going through another period of drought. In 1934 Nebraska approved the adoption of a unicameral state legislature—having only one house instead of the two that are used by the other 49 states.

Manufacturing, oil, and natural gas all became more important industries in Nebraska during World War II, and wartime food shortages were a boon to the state's farmers. Corn, wheat, oats, and potatoes were produced in record-breaking quantities. Today, Nebraska remains essentially an agricultural state, but its economy is shifting toward manufacturing, with emphasis on food products, machinery, metal goods, and electronics. Farms are consolidating, leading to fewer and larger farms. Its modern farming methods have increased production substantially. Since 1980, the cost of farm operations has risen as market prices have remained low and land prices have fallen. Numerous Nebraska farmers are in debt because a sharp decline in income has kept them from paying these debts on loans acquired in the mid-1970s. As a result, many farmers have been forced out of business. In 1982, Initiative 300 was adopted. This amendment to the state constitution prohibits corporations from acquiring farm or ranch land in the state. Initiative 300 was instituted to maintain the family farm, but it has been criticized for keeping land prices down and slowing the development of corporation-owned feed lots.

Education

Nebraskans have always been vitally interested in education. After the first school was established at Fort Atkinson, mission schools for the Indians were set up by various religious groups. The first legislature of the Nebraska Territory passed a free-school law in 1855. The first institution of higher education, Doane College, was established in 1858, nine years before Nebraska became a state. Higher education blossomed, and by the turn of the century, 11 more colleges and universities had been founded: Peru State College (1867), the University of Nebraska (1869), Creighton University (1878), Hastings College (1882), Dana College (1884), Midland Lutheran College (1883), Nebraska Wesleyan University (1887), Union College (1891), Wayne State College (1891), and Concordia Teachers College (1894). In 1963 the Nebraska Education Television Act was passed as Nebraska became one of the first states to offer substantial educational television (ETV) broadcasts.

Above:
Stage and screen actor Henry Fonda was a native of Grand Island, Nebraska. He often portrayed men of integrity and warmth in his more than 70 films.

Below:
Malcolm X, born Malcolm Little in Omaha, Nebraska, in 1925, was a prominent black activist during the 1960s. An aggressive and articulate speaker, Malcolm X was assassinated in February 1965, while addressing a rally in New York City.

The People

About 49 percent of Nebraskans live in metropolitan areas, and some 98 percent were born in the United States. Nebraska's largest communities include Omaha, Lincoln, Sioux City, Brownville, and Blair. Almost one-third of the state's population is of German descent. Protestants make up the largest religious group in the state, although there are many Roman Catholics, especially in urban areas. The largest Protestant body is the Lutheran Church; others include Baptists, Disciples of Christ, Episcopalians, Methodists, Presbyterians, and members of the United Church of Christ.

Famous People

Many famous people were born in the state of Nebraska. Here are a few:

Grover Cleveland Alexander 1887-1950, Elba. Hall of Fame baseball pitcher

Fred Astaire 1899-1987, Omaha. Dancer and film actor: *The Gay Divorcée, Silk Stockings*

Max Baer 1909-59, Omaha. Heavyweight boxing champion

Wade Boggs b. 1958, Omaha. Baseball player

Marlon Brando b. 1924, Omaha. Two-time Academy Award-winning actor: *On the Waterfront, The Godfather*

Montgomery Clift 1920-66, Omaha. Film actor: *Red River, From Here to Eternity*

Sam Crawford 1880-1968, Wahoo. Hall of Fame baseball player

Sandy Dennis 1937-92, Hastings. Academy Award–winning film actress: *Who's Afraid of Virginia Woolf?*

Henry Fonda 1905-82, Grand Island. Academy Award-winning film actor: *On Golden Pond, The Grapes of Wrath*

Gerald R. Ford b. 1913, Omaha. Thirty-eighth president of the United States

Bob Gibson b. 1935, Omaha. Hall of Fame baseball pitcher

Swoosie Kurtz b. 1944, Omaha. Tony Award-winning stage and television actress: *Sisters*

Harold Lloyd 1893-1971, Burchard. Actor and film producer

Malcolm X 1925-65, Omaha. Religious leader

Red Cloud 1822-1909, north-central Nebraska. Indian leader

Colleges and Universities

There are many colleges and universities in Nebraska. Here are the more prominent, with their locations, dates of founding, and undergraduate enrollments.

Bellevue College, Bellevue, 1965, 2,157

Chadron State College, Chadron, 1911, 2,850

College of Saint Mary, Omaha, 1923, 1,127

Concordia College, Seward, 1894, 870

Creighton University, Omaha, 1878, 5,600

Dana College, Blair, 1884, 542

Hastings College, Hastings, 1882, 1,016

Midland Lutheran College, Fremont, 1883, 962

Nebraska Wesleyan University, Lincoln, 1887, 1,694

Peru State College, Peru, 1867, 1,592

Union College, Lincoln, 1891, 576

University of Nebraska at Kearney, Kearney, 1903, 8,775; *at Omaha*, Omaha, 1908, 17,045; *at Lincoln*, Lincoln, 1869, 24,573; *Medical Center*, Omaha, 1869, 2,757

Wayne State College, Wayne, 1891, 3,761

Where To Get More Information

Nebraska Travel and
  Tourism Division
P.O. Box 94666
Lincoln, NE 68509
1-800-228-4307

North Dakota

The state seal of North Dakota, adopted in 1889, shows an elm tree surrounded by three sheaves of wheat, a plow, an anvil, and a sledge, representing agriculture. A bow, three arrows, and an Indian on horseback chasing a buffalo symbolize the tribes that lived in the region. The state motto and 42 stars appear in a semicircle around the top. In the border surrounding the seal is printed "Great Seal, State of North Dakota" and "October 1st, 1889."

NORTH DAKOTA
At a Glance

State Capital ★
Cities or towns ●
OF SPECIAL INTEREST ■

MINNESOTA

Grafton
ark River
Grand Forks
●Larimore

Mayville●

ey City
West Fargo ● **Fargo**

●Enderlin

●Lisbon

Wahpeton●

OTA

Capital: Bismarck

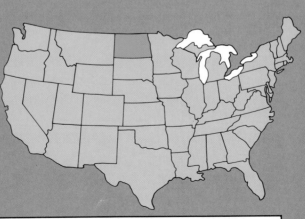

Size: 70,702 square miles (17th largest)
Population: 635,927 (47th largest)

State Flag

Major Industries:
Agriculture, livestock, mining, farm equipment, processed foods

Major Crops:
Grains, potatoes, soybeans

State Flower:
Wild Prairie Rose

State Flag

The state flag of North Dakota, adopted in 1911, contains a bald eagle with spread wings carrying an olive branch and arrows in its talons. In its beak is a scroll that reads *E Pluribus Unum* (one out of many). The design, centered on a blue background, resembles the coat of arms of the United States. A scroll with the state name appears at the bottom of the flag. Above the eagle is a double semicircle of stars representing the original 13 states.

State Motto

Liberty and Union, Now and Forever, One and Inseparable

This quotation from Daniel Webster's "Reply to Hayne" was adopted as state motto in 1889.

Lake Sakakawea is one of many that dot the North Dakota landscape.

State Capital

Bismarck became the territorial capital in 1883 and the state capital in 1889, when North Dakota entered the Union.

State Name and Nicknames

North Dakota was named for the Sioux Indians, who called themselves *Dakota* or *Lakota,* which meant "allies" or "friends."

North Dakota's two official nicknames are the *Sioux State* and the *Flickertail State.* They refer to the Sioux Indians that inhabited the area and to the state's large population of flickertail ground squirrels. North Dakota is also known as the *Peace Garden State* for the International Peace Garden, which lies on its border with Manitoba.

State Flower

In 1907, the state legislature selected the wild prairie rose, *Rosa blanda* or *Rosa arkansana,* as state flower.

State Tree

The American elm, *Ulmus americana,* was chosen state tree in 1947.

State Bird

The western meadowlark, *Sturnella neglecta,* was designated state bird in 1947.

State Art Gallery

In 1981, the University of North Dakota Art Gallery, on the Grand Forks campus, was selected state art gallery.

State Beverage

Milk was named state beverage in 1983.

State Fossil

Teredo petrified wood was chosen state fossil in 1967.

State Grass

In 1977, western wheat grass, *Agropyron smithii,* was designated state grass.

State March

In 1975, "Spirit of the Land," written by James D. Ployhar, was adopted as state march.

State Song

"North Dakota Hymn," with words by James W. Foley and music by C. S. Putnam, was named state song in 1947.

Population

The population of North Dakota in 1992 was 635,927, making it the 47th most populous state. There are 9.03 people per square mile. Approximately 40 percent of North Dakotans live in metropolitan areas, with the largest urban areas at Fargo, Grand Forks, Minot, and Bismarck.

About 98 percent of North Dakotans were born in the United States; those born in foreign countries came mainly from Canada, Germany, Norway, and Russia. The earliest Indian peoples to live in North Dakota were the Mandan, Hidatsa, and Arikara along the Missouri River, the Chippewa and Cree in the northeast, the Assinboin in the north, the Yanktonia Sioux and Wahpeton Dakota in the southeast and the Teton Sioux and Crow in the west. The French, English, Canadians, and Scots were attracted to this area by the fur trade, and by 1800 the Métis—of mixed white and Indian ancestry—were common in the region. Today, Native Americans compose approximately 3 percent of the total population, and they comprise the largest minority group in North Dakota. Many Indians have established successful careers as professionals, athletes, politicians, farmers, and ranchers. More than half of the church members in the state belong to the Lutheran Church and over one-third are Roman Catholics.

Industries

The principal industries of the state are agriculture, mining, manufacturing, and tourism. The chief manufactured products are farm equipment, and processed foods.

The Badlands were created over three million years by water flooding soft sediments and volcanic ash.

Agriculture

The chief crops of the state are spring wheat, durum, barley, rye, flaxseed, oats, potatoes, dried edible beans, honey, soybeans, sugar beets, sunflowers, and hay. North Dakota is also a livestock state; there are estimated to be 1.85 million cattle, 290,000 hogs and pigs, 214,000 sheep, and 1.5 million chickens and turkeys on its farms. Lime, construction sand and gravel, and crushed stone are important mineral resources.

Government

The governor is elected to a four-year term, as are the lieutenant governor, attorney general, secretary of state, treasurer, auditor, and superintendent of public instruction. The state legislature, which meets in odd-numbered years, consists of a 53-member senate and a 106-member house of representatives. Forty-nine of the 53 legislative districts elect one senator and two representatives. For voting purposes, the remaining four are grouped into two districts, each of which elects two senators and four representatives. Senators serve four-year terms, and representatives serve two-year terms. In addition to its two United States senators, North Dakota has one representative in the U. S. House of Representatives. The state has three votes in the electoral college.

Sports

Many sporting events on the collegiate and secondary school levels are played throughout the state. In hockey, the University of North Dakota won the NCAA championship in 1959, 1963, 1980, 1982, and 1987.

Major Cities

Bismarck (population 49,272). Founded in 1873 as

Fort Totten is a well-preserved frontier military outpost that was established on the shore of Devils Lake in July 1867.

the Western terminus of the Northern Pacific trans-continental railroad, the town was named in honor of Germany's "Iron" chancellor in an effort to attract German investors for the railroad. The capital city of North Dakota, which lies on the east bank of the Missouri River, developed into an important riverboat port and railway terminal. In 1876, the port

The International Peace Garden is located in the Turtle Mountains on the border of the Canadian province of Manitoba. It symbolizes the long relationship between the United States and Canada.

served as a supply point for General George Custer's ill-fated expedition against the Indians in Montana. Bismarck became the capital of the Dakota Territory in 1883. When the territory was divided into North and South Dakota and the two states were admitted to the Union in 1889, Bismarck became the capital of North Dakota. Since the first oil well opened in 1951, Bismarck has become a center for this growing industry.

Things to see in Bismarck:
State Capitol, North Dakota Heritage Center, State Historical Museum, Statue of Sakakawea, Camp Hancock State Historic Site, Riverside-Sertoma Park, Dakota Zoo, Double Ditch Indian Village, and E'lan Art Gallery.

Fargo (population 74,084). Founded in 1872, North Dakota's largest city is located in the fertile Red River Valley. It is a leading commercial center of the Northwest. The city, named for William G. Fargo of the Wells Fargo Express

Bitter cold winters are not uncommon in North Dakota, which averages 37 inches of snow per year.

Company, became important as a supply point for settlers headed west. Many of Fargo's hotels feature casinos run by charities and nonprofit organizations.

Things to see in Fargo:
Roger Maris Baseball Museum, and Bonanzaville, USA.

The spirit of the West is alive at Frontier Village in Jamestown, where visitors can see a collection of 19th-century buildings.

Grand Forks (population 49,417). Originally called "Les Grandes Fourches" by French explorers, this trading post of the North West Company was situated here in 1801. The first permanent settlement was started in 1871. It was organized in 1879 and later became a station on the Great Northern Railway in 1880. Today it is the main trade center for the Red River valley, an area which produces potatoes, beets, sugar, small grains, and raises various types of livestock. It continues to be an important transportation center for railroads, highways, and the municipal airport which is an international point of entry.

Places to Visit

The National Park Service maintains three areas in the state of North Dakota: Theodore Roosevelt National Park, Knife River Indian Villages National Historic Site, and part of Fort Union Trading Post National Historic Site. In addition, there are 12 state recreation areas.

Bottineau: International Peace Garden. Located in the Turtle Mountains on both sides of the United States-Canadian border, this complex is a tribute to the friendship of the two nations.

Devils Lake: Fort Totten State Historic Site. The 1867 fort, built to protect settlers headed for Montana, contains many of the original buildings.

Grand Forks: Myra Museum and Campbell House. The museum, featuring artifacts from the late-19th century, shares the grounds with the 1879 log cabin home of agricultural innovator Tom Campbell.

Jamestown: Frontier Village. The "World's Largest Buffalo," a three-story statue of an American bison, is the main feature of this complex, which also contains many restored buildings.

Mandan: Fort Abraham Lincoln State Park. The reconstructed Commanding Officer's Quarters, the home of General George A. Custer from 1873-76, is located on the park grounds.

Rugby: Geographical Center Pioneer Village and Museum. The village, which features 27 restored buildings, stands at the geographical center of the North American continent.

Events

There are many events and organizations that schedule activities of various kinds in the state of North Dakota. Here are some of them.

Sports: Badlands Circuit Finals Rodeo (Bismarck), McQuades Softball Tournament (Bismarck), Sports Camp (Bottineau), Roger Maris Celebrity Golf Tournament (Fargo), Governor's Walleye Cup Derby (Garrison), State Hockey Tournament (Grand Forks), Potato Bowl (Grand Forks), Fort Abraham Lincoln Great American Horse Race (Mandan), Rodeo Days (Mandan), Champions Ride Rodeo (Sentinel Butte), Winter Carnival (Williston).

Arts and Crafts: Summerthing (Grand Forks), Spring Craft Show (Jamestown), Art in the Park (Mandan), Country Fair (Rugby).

Music: Summer Pops Series (Bismarck), International Music Camp (Bottineau), Phil Patterson Bandshell Concerts (Dickinson), International Old Time Fiddlers' Contest (Dunseith), Medora Musical (Medora), Frost Fire Musical (Walhalla), Band Day (Williston).

Entertainment: Missouri River Expo (Bismarck), Missouri Valley Fair (Bismarck), United Tribes Pow-Wow (Bismarck), Folkfest

The United Tribes Pow-Wow celebrates North Dakota's Native American heritage.

(Bismarck), Waterski Carnival (Bottineau), Steam Thresher Show (Carrington), Carrington Folkfest (Carrington), Fort Totten Days (Devils Lake), Roughrider Days Celebration (Dickinson), Pioneer Days (Dickinson), Northern Plains Ethnic Festival (Dickinson), Heritage Hjemkomst Festival (Fargo), Merry Prairie Christmas (Fargo), Sodbuster Days (Fort Ransom), Native American Annual Time Out and Wacipi (Grand Forks), Potato Bowl Week (Grand Forks), Stutsman County Fair (Jamestown), Buffalo Days (Jamestown), Frontier Army Days (Mandan), Winter Daze (Mandan), North Dakota State Fair (Minot), Norsk Hostfest (Minot), Little Shell

Powwow (New Town), Turtle Mountain Pow-Wow Celebration (Rolla), State Championship Horse Show (Rugby), North Dakota Winter Show (Valley City), Community Days (Valley City), Fort Buford 6th Infantry State Historical Encampment (Williston), Fort Union Trading Post Rendezvous (Williston), Buffalo Trails Day (Williston), Samlingfest (Williston).

Tours: Lewis and Clark Riverboat (Bismarck), Dakota Queen Riverboat (Grand Forks), Yard and Garden Tour (Hatton), Fort Seward Wagon Train (Jamestown).

Theater: Fort Totten Little Theatre (Devils Lake), LaMoure Summer Theatre (Grand Rapids).

The Land and the Climate

North Dakota is bounded on the west by Montana, on the north by the Canadian provinces of Saskatchewan and Manitoba, on the east by Minnesota, and on the south by South Dakota. The state has three major land divisions: the Red River Valley, the Young Drift Plains, and the Great Plains.

The Red River Valley is a narrow strip along the Minnesota border. It is part of an ancient glacial lake bed and has extremely fertile soil that supports dairy farms and fields of wheat, barley, rye, flax, sugar beets, soybeans, and oats. This is North Dakota's most populous area.

The Young Drift Plains are west of the Red River Valley and rise gradually toward the west and southwest. They comprise low hills o earth materials left by the glaciers (called drift) and stream-cut valleys. The Turtle Mountains are located in the northern section. This is a region of grain farms, cattle and dairy farms, and some oil wells and coal mines.

The Great Plains cover the southwestern half of the state. They are
art of the huge highland that runs from Canada to southern Texas.
North Dakota they are also called the Missouri Plateau. The
gion's hills provide good grazing for cattle and sheep. Wheat fields
e found here, as well as rich mineral deposits—uranium, natural
as, and oil.

In the southwest are the Badlands—a valley of sandstone, shale,
d clay filled with weird rock formations carved by natural forces.
ench traders named them "bad-for-traveling."

The most important river systems in North Dakota are those of the
issouri and Red Rivers. The state has hundreds of small lakes,
pecially in the Young Drift Plains. One of the most unusual is
evils Lake, which has no outlet and contains water that is slightly
lty.

Bitter-cold, snowy winters and warm, sunny summers are typical
the weather in North Dakota. Low humidity keeps the state cool
summer, in spite of the long hours of sunshine (North Dakota has
ore hours of sunlight per day than any other state). Average
mperatures in July are 71 degrees Fahrenheit, and in January, 10
grees F. Snowfall averages 37 inches per year and rain is most
equent between April and September—some 18 inches per year.

Above:
Lake Sakakawea, which
covers 609 miles in the
western half of North Dakota,
is one of the world's largest
man-made lakes. The Missouri
River supplies its waters,
which are contained by
Garrison Dam, a huge earth-
fill dam and hydroelectric-
power complex.

At left:
The sun sets over North
Dakota's vast, flat prairies,
which typify the landscape of
the state.

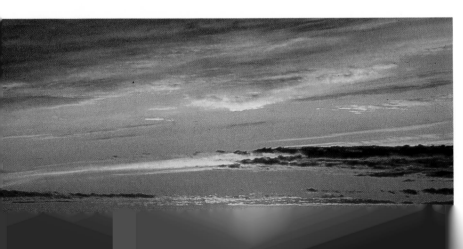

The Great Plains, also called the Missouri Plateau in North Dakota, provide excellent grazing for livestock. Millions of buffalo roamed the vast sweep of land for centuries until the mid-1800s, when they were hunted almost to extinction by whites. At the same time, the U.S. Army was driv-

g Native American tribes in the area
nto reservations to make room for white set-
ers. These homesteaders established wheat
rms and cattle ranches that quickly succeeded
 the rich land. While agriculture is still central
 the state's economy, in recent years North
akota has developed its mineral resources and
s industries.

At right:
A Mandan warrior performing the ceremonial Dog Dance. The Mandan were primarily an agricultural people, who were farming the North Dakota region when French explorers arrived.

Far right:
A portrait of a Hidatsa chief, who led one of the many Indian tribes native to the North Dakota region. The Hidatsa, Mandan, Arikara, Sioux, Assiniboin, and Cheyenne were among the territory's first inhabitants.

The History

Most original inhabitants of what is now North Dakota were peaceful farmers living in the Missouri Valley in the south-central part of the territory. They belonged to the Arikara, Cheyenne, Hidatsa, and Mandan tribes and lived in villages that were fortified for protection from raids by the hunter and warrior tribes that occasionally came down from the northeast, such as the Assiniboin, Chippewa, and Sioux, or Dakota. After they acquired horses, which had been introduced to Central America by the Spanish *conquistadores* in the late 16th century, farming became less important. The northern Plains people became buffalo hunters like the other tribes in the region.

In 1682 the explorer Robert Cavelier (known as La Salle) claimed for France all lands along the Mississippi River and its tributaries, including the southwestern half of present-day North Dakota, whence the Missouri River flows into the Mississippi. France also laid claim to the northeastern part of the region as an extension of its Hudson Bay holdings in Canada. In 1713 France ceded the Hudson Bay territory to Great Britain.

The North Dakota area was not explored until 1738, when the French fur trader Pierre de la Vérendrye set out from Canada and reached the Mandan Indian village near present-day Bismarck. After the Louisiana Purchase of 1803, President Thomas Jefferson sent Meriwether Lewis and William Clark on their famous expedition to explore the vast territory formerly held by France. They reached central North Dakota in October 1804 and built Fort Mandan on the east bank of the Missouri River, opposite present-day Stanton. Scottish and Irish families from Canada began emigrating to North Dakota, and in 1812 they founded a settlement at Pembina. Four years later the United States obtained northeastern North Dakota from Great Britain by treaty, and by 1823 Pembina was deserted: the settlers moved back to Canada in order to remain under British rule.

It wasn't until 1861 that Congress created the Dakota Territory, which included what is now North and South Dakota and much of Montana and Wyoming. Even then, the lack of roads and railroads and fear of Indians, especially the Sioux, kept homesteaders away. During the 1860s and the 1870s, federal troops suppressed Indian uprisings against seizure of their lands and treaties broken by the government. Peace did not return until 1881, when Sioux chief Sitting Bull surrendered to U.S. soldiers.

The turning point came about 1875, when eastern businesses and enterprising settlers established enormous wheat farms of from 3,000 to 65,000 acres, mainly in the Red River Valley. They were so successful that they were nicknamed "bonanza" farms, and stories

Sacagawea, the Shoshone woman who acted as a guide and interpreter for the explorers Lewis and Clark, joined their expedition in North Dakota in 1804. Although she set out from Fort Mandan with a month-old baby and fell sick several times, Sacagawea made the year-long journey to Oregon's Fort Clatsop and Tillamook Head. She was the only woman on the Lewis and Clark Expedition.

Fort Abercrombie, built in the southern Red River Valley in 1857, was the first military post constructed in North Dakota. Similar forts were built during this time to protect supply lines and assist pioneers, as they pushed the Indians farther west in their effort to settle the land.

about them brought thousands of settlers into the region. Because towns were growing up in distant corners of the huge Dakota Territory, where communication and transportation were difficult, settlers requested that it be divided in half. This division took place in 1889, and later that year the states of North and South Dakota were admitted to the Union. North Dakota became the 39th state.

The population of North Dakota more than doubled between 1890 and 1910, but the farmers still had to deal with Minnesota banks, grain companies, and railroads. In 1915 the Nonpartisan League was formed, which advocated state ownership of large farming facilities like grain elevators and storage plants. In 1919 the Bank of North Dakota was established, and in 1922 the North Dakota Mill and Elevator in Grand Forks began operating.

North Dakota was severely affected by the Great Depression of the 1930s, when farm production declined, residents began leaving the state, and a severe drought occurred. State and national programs to promote irrigation projects and prevent soil erosion helped farmers regain their productivity. The United States entered World War II in in 1941, and North Dakota excelled in meeting the armed forces's need for farm products. The war brought jobs to many unemployed North Dakotans. At the same time, there was sufficient rainfall during these years, resulting in good crop yields and increased farm prices and land values. North Dakota also profited as agricultural production was mechanized, chemical pesticides and fertilizers were introduced, and plant and animal varieties were improved. Oil was discovered near Tioga in 1951, and it soon became North Dakota's most valuable mineral resource. Today, the state is moving away from its traditional dependence on agriculture and making a determined effort to foster industry. Its principal manufactured goods are farm equipment and processed foods, and vast coal fields are an important source of power. An economic development commission was created in 1957 to encourage industry to come to the state. Now over 80 North Dakota communities have their own development commissions. As

The rugged spirit of the plains and prairies is captured by bull riding, one of the state's most popular rodeo events.

a result, from 1958-69, North Dakota had the highest industrial growth rate in the country.

North Dakota continues to work to attract industries to the state. The availability of nonagricultural jobs has been increasing, but not fast enough to match the decline in agricultural jobs. This is a difficult task due to North Dakota's location distant from the nation's largest population centers.

A traditional Scandinavian festival. Settlers from Norway and other Scandinavian countries were among the first to farm and build on North Dakota soil. Other immigrants came from Germany and Russia.

Education

The first school in North Dakota was established by Roman Catholic missionaries at Pembina in 1818. Public schools were mandated by the government of the Dakota Territory in 1862. A number of rural elementary and high schools are too small to offer all of the traditional programs. Even into the late 1980s, there were 12 high schools with 20 or fewer students enrolled. The first institution of higher education, the University of North Dakota, was founded in 1883.

Famous People

Many famous people were born in or relocated to North Dakota. Here are a few:

Fred G. Aandahl 1897-1966, Litchville. U.S. government official

Lynn Anderson b. 1947, Grand Forks. Country and pop singer

Maxwell Anderson 1888-1959, Pennsylvania. Playwright

Henry Luke Bolley 1865-1956, Indiana. Botanist

George Catlin 1796-1872, Pennsylvania. Western Indian expert and artist

Charles Turner Cavileer c.1818-1902, North Dakota. First permanent white settler in North Dakota

Angie Dickinson b. 1931, Kulm. Television and film actress: *Police Woman, Dressed to Kill*

Roy Sarles Durstine 1886-1962, Jamestown. Advertising executive

Carl Ben Eielson 1897-1929, Hatton. Bush pilot

John B. Flannagan 1895-1942, Fargo. Sculptor

Croil Hunter 1893-1970, Fargo. Airline executive

Edwin F. Ladd 1859-1925, Maine. U.S. senator and farmer

Louis L'Amour 1908-88, Jamestown. Novelist

William Langer 1886-1959, near Everest. Senate leader

Peggy Lee b. 1920, Jamestown. Pop singer

Clement H. Lounsberry 1843-1926, Indiana. Editor and correspondent; established *Bismarck Tribune*

Roger Maris 1934-1985, Minnesota. Baseball player

Pete Retzlaff b. 1931, Ellendale. Football player

Eric Sevareid 1912-92, Velva. Newscaster

Linda W. Slaughter 1843-1911, Ohio. Author, composer, and lecturer who organized the first school in Bismarck in 1870

Ann Sothern b. 1909, Valley City. Television and film actress: *The Ann Sothern Show, The Whales of August*

Lawrence Welk 1903-92, near Strasburg. Bandleader

Colleges and Universities

There are many colleges and universities in North Dakota. Here are the more prominent, with their locations, dates of founding, and undergraduate enrollments.

Dickinson State College, Dickinson, 1918, 1,605

Jamestown College, Jamestown, 1884, 1,083

Mayville State University, Mayville, 1889, 665

Minot State College, Minot, 1913, 3,797

North Dakota State University, Fargo, 1890, 9,307

University of Mary, Bismarck, 1959, 1,287

University of North Dakota, Grand Forks, 1883, 12,438

Valley City State College, Valley City, 1889, 1,003

Where To Get More Information

Tourism Promotion Division
Economic Development
Commission
Liberty Memorial building
600 E. Boulevard Avenue
Bismarck, ND 58505
1-800-437-2077

South Dakota

The state seal of South Dakota, adopted in 1889, depicts a landscape with a farmer plowing, a steamboat on the river, a smelter furnace, and cattle grazing in a field of corn. Hills can be seen in the distance, and the state motto appears on a scroll at the top. The border inscription reads "State of South Dakota, Great Seal" and "1889," the year the state joined the Union.

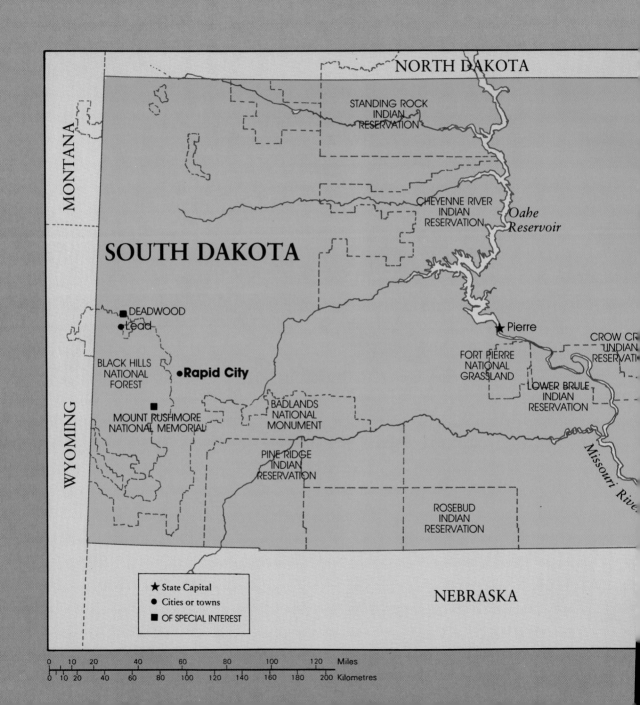

NORTH DAKOTA

MONTANA

STANDING ROCK
INDIAN
RESERVATION

CHEYENNE RIVER
INDIAN
RESERVATION

*Oahe
Reservoir*

SOUTH DAKOTA

■DEADWOOD
●Lead

★Pierre

CROW CR
INDIAN
RESERVATI

BLACK HILLS
NATIONAL
FOREST

●**Rapid City**

FORT PIERRE
NATIONAL
GRASSLAND

LOWER BRULE
INDIAN
RESERVATION

■
MOUNT RUSHMORE
NATIONAL MEMORIAL

BADLANDS
NATIONAL
MONUMENT

WYOMING

PINE RIDGE
INDIAN
RESERVATION

Missouri River

ROSEBUD
INDIAN
RESERVATION

★ State Capital
● Cities or towns
■ OF SPECIAL INTEREST

NEBRASKA

| 0 | 10 | 20 | 40 | 60 | 80 | 100 | 120 | Miles |

| 0 | 10 | 20 | 40 | 60 | 80 | 100 | 120 | 140 | 160 | 180 | 200 | Kilometres |

SOUTH DAKOTA

At a Glance

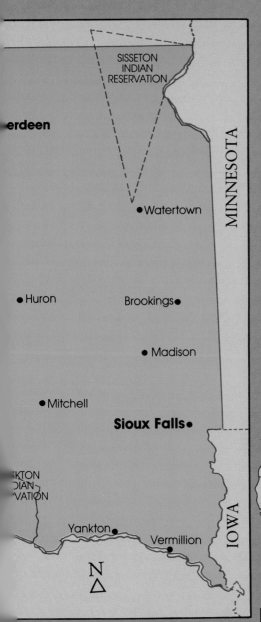

State Flower:
American Pasqueflower

State Bird:
Ring-necked Pheasant

Capital: Pierre

Major Industries: Agriculture, clothing, machinery, glass products, livestock

Major Crops: Wheat, corn, oats, hay, rye

State Flag

Size: 77,116 square miles (16th largest)
Population: 711,154 (45th largest)

State Flag

South Dakota has two official state flags. The first, adopted in 1909, contains the state seal on one side and the sun on the other. Because of the expense involved in manufacturing a two-sided flag, a second was adopted in 1963. It consists of the state seal surrounded by a yellow sunburst and the words "South Dakota—The Sunshine State," centered on a sky blue field.

State Motto

Under God the People Rule
This motto, originally adopted in 1885, was suggested by Dr. Joseph Ward, founder of Yankton College.

The 60-foot-high faces of four great presidents—Washington, Jefferson, Theodore Roosevelt, and Lincoln—grace the majestic Black Hills that are the backdrop of Mount Rushmore.

State Capital
 Pierre was selected as the temporary capital when South Dakota became a state in 1889. It was named the permanent capital in 1904.

State Name and Nicknames
 The name South Dakota

One of the best trout streams in the Black Hills rolls through Spearfish Canyon.

came from the Sioux Indians of the region, who called themselves *Dakota* or *Lakota*, meaning "allies" or "friends."
 South Dakota is nicknamed the *Sunshine State* because of its sunny climate. It has also been called the *Coyote State* for its many coyotes. Other nicknames include the *Blizzard State* because of its harsh winters and the *Artesian State* for its many artesian wells.

State Flower
 The American pasque flower, *Pulsatilla hirsutissima*, was chosen state flower in 1903.

State Tree
 The Black Hills spruce, *Picea glauca densata*, was adopted as state tree in 1947.

State Bird
 In 1943, the ring-necked pheasant, *Phasianus colchicus*, was named state bird by the legislature.

State Animal
 The coyote was designated state animal in 1949.

State Fish
 The walleye, *Stizostedion vitreum*, was selected state fish in 1982.

State Gem
 In 1966, fairburn agate was chosen state gem.

State Grass
 Western wheat grass, *Agropyron smithii*, was adopted state grass in 1970.

State Insect
 The honeybee, *apis mellifera*, was named state insect in 1978.

State Mineral
 Rose quartz was selected state mineral in 1966.

State Song
 "Hail, South Dakota," words and music by Deecort Hammitt, was adopted state song in 1943.

Population

The population of South Dakota in 1992 was 711,154, making it the 45th most populous state. There are 90.2 people per square mile.

Industries

The principal industries of the state are agriculture, manufacturing, and services. The chief manufactured products are food and food products, machinery, and electric and electronic equipment.

Agriculture

The chief crops of the state are corn, oats, wheat, sunflowers, soybeans, and sorghum. South Dakota is also a livestock state; there are estimated to be 3.75 million cattle, 1.8 million hogs and pigs, and 591,000 sheep on its farms. Ponderosa pine is harvested. Gold and Portland cement are important mineral resources.

Government

The governor is elected to a four-year term, as are the lieutenant governor, secretary of state, attorney general, commissioner of school and public lands, treasurer, and auditor. The state legislature, which meets annually, consists of a 35-member senate and a 70-member house of representatives. Voters in each of the 35 legislative districts elect one senator and two representatives for two-year terms.

In addition to its two United States senators, South Dakota has one representative in the U.S. House of Representatives. The state has three votes in the electoral college.

Sports

The Rapid City Thrillers and the Sioux Falls Skyforce are members of the Continental Basketball Association, the official developmental league of the National Basketball Association. In addition, hiking, fishing, and water sports are also popular.

Major Cities

Rapid City (population 54,523). Originally inhabited by Sioux Indians, it was founded by white settlers in 1876, two years after the discovery of gold in the Black Hills. Rapid City is the second largest city in the state. It is named after Rapid Creek, which flows through Rapid City. Tourism, mining, lumbering, and agriculture support the local economy.

Needles Highway was built to showcase the striking rock formations of the Black Hills.

Things to see in Rapid City:
Sioux Indian Museum and Crafts Center, Minnilusa Pioneer Museum, Dahl Fine Arts Center, Dinosaur Park, South Dakota School of Mines and Technology, Museum of Geology, Stage Barn Crystal Cave, Black Hills Petrified Forest, Crystal Cave Park, Sitting Bull Crystal Cave, Black Hills Caverns, Marine Life Aquarium, Story Book Island, Black Hills Reptile Gardens, Thunderhead Underground Falls, Chapel in the Hills, Ellsworth Air Force Base, and Bear Country, USA

Sioux Falls (population 100,836). Originally founded in 1856, the town was abandoned six years later because of the threat of attacks by the Minnesota Sioux Indians. It is named for the falls of the Sioux River. It was reestablished as Fort Dakota in 1865 and prospered. In 1873 the falls were controlled and utilized for water power. Due to lax divorce laws, Sioux Falls became famous as a "divorce mill" from 1890-1910. The eastern border of Sioux Falls houses one of the world's first commercial nuclear power plants, and its stockyards are one of the largest livestock markets in the United States.

Things to see in Sioux Falls:
Pettigrew Home and Museum, Old Courthouse Museum, E.R.O.S. Data Center, Sherman Park, Great Plains Zoo, Delbridge Museum of Natural History, Indian Mounds, USS *South Dakota* Battleship Memorial, Civic Fine Arts Center/Museum, and the Center for Western Studies.

Places to Visit

The National Park Service maintains four areas in the state of South Dakota: Mount Rushmore National Memorial, Jewel Cave National Monument, Wind Cave National Park, and Badlands National Park. In addition, there are 29 state recreation areas.

Custer: National Museum of Woodcarving. The museum features life-size animated figures by Dr. Niblack, one of

Mammoth Site in Hot Springs holds one of the largest collections of prehistoric elephant fossils in the Western Hemisphere.

the original animators of Disneyland.

Deadwood: Ghosts of Deadwood Gulch Wax Museum. More than 70 wax figures portray historic scenes in the settlement of South Dakota.

De Smet: Laura Ingalls Wilder Memorial. Guided tours of this area include the author's childhood home and many other buildings referred to in her books.

Hot Springs: Mammoth Site. This excavation site contains the largest known concentration of mammoth bones in the Western Hemisphere.

Huron: Gladys Pyle Historic Home. This Queen Anne style house, built around 1894, was the home of the first woman elected to the U.S. Senate.

Keystone: Rushmore-Borglum Story and Gallery. Exhibits include original models and tools used by Gutzon Borglum in sculpting Mount Rushmore.

Lead: The Homestake Gold Mine. Visitors may tour the surface workings of one of the largest operating gold mines in the Western Hemisphere.

Mitchell: Enchanted World Doll Museum. This museum—a castle with a drawbridge, moat, and stained-glass windows—houses more than 4,000 dolls arranged in scenes from fairy tales and story books.

Pierre: South Dakota Discovery Center and Aquarium. Hands-on exhibits in many areas allow visitors to discover and experiment with science.

Spearfish: Classic Auto Museum.

Exhibits include more than 100 antique and classic cars dating from 1908 to the 1960s.

Events

There are many events and organizations that schedule activities of various kinds in the state of South Dakota. Here are some of them.

Sports: Black Hills Roundup (Belle Fourche), State Fair Speedway (Huron), Corn Palace Stampede Rodeo (Mitchell), Greyhound Racing at Black Hills Greyhound Track (Rapid City), Black Hills Motorcycle Classic (Sturgis), Pro-Bowl Rodeo (Watertown), Elks Rodeo (Winner).

Arts and Crafts: Summer Festival (Brookings), Meadowood Arts Fair (Huron), Black Hills Gold (Rapid City), Sioux Pottery and Crafts (Rapid City), Black Hills Pow Wow and Arts Expo (Rapid City), Northern Plains Tribal Arts (Sioux Falls).

Music: Mountain Music Show (Custer), Fife and Drum Corp Concerts (Hill City), South Dakota and Open Fiddling Contest (Yankton).

Entertainment: Snow Queen Festival (Aberdeen), Little International (Brookings), Gold Discovery Days (Custer), Fall

Festival (Custer), Days of '76 (Deadwood), Heart of the Hills Celebration (Hill City), Huron Air Show (Huron), South Dakota State Fair (Huron), Steam Threshing Jamboree (Madison), Corn Palace Festival (Mitchell), Corn Palace Polka Festival (Mitchell), Oglala Nation Fair and Rodeo (Pine Ridge), Black Hills Heritage Festival (Rapid City), Central States Fair (Rapid City), Rosebud Sioux Tribal Affairs and Powwow (Rosebud), Sioux Empire Fair (Sioux Falls), Fort Sisseton Historical Festival (Sisseton), Antique Auto Festival (Sisseton), Black Hills Sawdust Day (Spearfish), Spring Festival (Sturgis), Steam and Gas Threshing Bee (Sturgis), Kampeska Days (Watertown), Wildlife Festival (Watertown), Day County Fair (Webster), Heritage Days (Yankton), Riverboat Days (Yankton).

Tours: Native American Loop (Chamberlain), Jeep Ride to Buffalo (Custer), Pickler Mansion (Faulkton), 1880 Train (Hill City), Homestake Gold Mine Surface Tours (Lead).

Theater: Trial of Jack McCall for the Murder of Wild Bill Hickok (Deadwood), Laura Ingalls Wilder Pageant (Huron), Black Hills Passion Play (Spearfish), Lewis and Clark Playhouse (Yankton).

The Land and the Climate

South Dakota's Badlands are in the southwestern part of the state. Named for their tough terrain and difficulty of passage, the Badlands have intricate, multicolored rock formations carved by wind and water erosion. They are surrounded by a series of plateaus and studded with tall buttes and pyramids.

Corn, wheat, oats, and sunflowers are South Dakota's most important and valuable crops.

South Dakota is bounded on the west by Montana and Wyoming, o the north by North Dakota, on the east by Minnesota and Iowa, an on the south by Nebraska. There are four major land divisions in th state: the Young Drift Plains, the Dissected Till Plains, the Great Plains, and the Black Hills.

The Young Drift Plains stretch over most of eastern South Dakot consisting of rolling hills and glacially formed lakes. This is cattle country, although many acres are given over to wheat farming.

The Dissected Till Plains form a loop in the southeastern corner o South Dakota. After the last glacier receded, streams began to cut u (dissect) till—soil, rocks, and other materials—deposited by the glaciers. The land here is good for raising beef and dairy cattle, poultry, and sheep, as well as corn, rye, hay, and oats.

The Great Plains cover most of the western two-thirds of the stat and include the Badlands—rough regions made up of steep hills and deep gullies worn by wind and water. The Badlands have little economic use, but most of the Great Plains region supports cattle, sheep, and wheat. Uranium, coal, and feldspar are also mined here.

The Black Hills region consists of a low, isolated mountain group
west-central South Dakota. It is a land of great scenic beauty, with
eep canyons; towering, rugged rock formations; and pine and
pruce forests. There are rich mineral deposits, including gold, clay,
ravel, and sand. The highest point east of the Rockies, 7,242-foot
arney Peak, is located in the Black Hills.

The most important river in South Dakota is the Missouri. Most of
he state's lakes were dug by glaciers during the Ice Age. One of the
ost interesting is Medicine Lake, near Florence, which has a salt
oncentration of about four percent—higher than that of sea water.

Extremes in temperature are not uncommon in South Dakota, but
ven in the hottest weather, low humidity keeps the air comfortable.
emperatures often go to 100 degrees Fahrenheit in the summer and
rop below 0 degrees F. in winter. The averages, however, are 74
egrees F. in July and 15 degrees F. in January. Rainfall is higher east
f the Missouri, and snowfall is heaviest during February and March.

Above:
Rapid City, on the eastern
edge of the Black Hills, is the
second largest city in South
Dakota.

At left:
The combination of rolling
prairies, steep rock
formations, and jagged cliffs
creates a dramatic landscape
in South Dakota. The state
flower, the pasqueflower,
flourishes in its rugged
surroundings.

The History

Before the white man came to what is now South Dakota, there wei three major Indian tribes living in the region. The Arikara were farmers who lived near the mouth of the Cheyenne River and north of it along the Missouri. In the western part of the Cheyenne River area were the Cheyenne, farmers and hunters, who were also active along the White River and in the Black Hills. The Sioux, or Dakota were nomadic hunters and warriors who followed the buffalo herds

When Robert Cavelier (known as La Salle) claimed all the lands drained by the Mississippi River system in 1682, France owned what would become South Dakota. Probably the first white men to explore the territory were the French-Canadians François and Louis Joseph de la Vérendrye, the sons of explorer Pierre de la Vérendrye. In 1743 these brothers buried an inscribed lead plate near present-day Fort Pierre to prove they had been there. This plate was not found until 1913, when schoolchildren discovered it.

In 1762 France ceded its land west of the Mississippi River to Spain, which returned it in 1800. Three years later the United State: bought this vast Louisiana Territory from France, and President Thomas Jefferson sent Meriwether Lewis and William Clark on the famous exploratory trip to the Pacific Ocean. In August of 1804, Lewis and Clark camped in the South Dakota region, near what is now Elk Point, and then went on to follow the Missouri River through the territory.

After the Lewis and Clark expedition, many fur trappers entered the region, and the first permanent settlement, a trading post, was built on the site of present-day Fort Pierre in 1817. It was establishe by Joseph la Framboise, a French trader. Despite troubles with the Indians, which began in 1823 and lasted into the 1830s, the fur trac thrived until the 1850s, when it suffered from both dwindling suppl and declining demand. During the years from 1812 to 1834, the are was part of the Missouri Territory.

An old gold mine still stands as a reminder of the great South Dakota gold rush of 1874, when gold was discovered in the Black Hills by General George Armstrong Custer and his men. In the fall of 1875, after the military ceased to uphold the treaty prohibiting white settlement in the Black Hills territory sacred to the Sioux, gold seekers poured into the area and quickly uprooted the Sioux, who surrendered their claims in 1876 after a series of uprisings.

At left:
Explorers Lewis and Clark greet Indians met on their way across the Great Plains. After President Thomas Jefferson concluded the Louisiana Purchase in 1803, he dispatched the Lewis and Clark Expedition to explore the territory. As the explorers made their journey to the Pacific, they passed through what is now South Dakota.

Below:
Calamity Jane, born Martha Jane Cannary, is perhaps America's most famous frontierswoman. At the height of South Dakota's "gold fever" in 1876, Jane arrived at Camp Deadwood, the most notorious of the lawless mining camps that dotted the Black Hills. There, she gambled at the poker tables, reputedly became Wild Bill Hickok's sweetheart, and performed in the Wild West shows.

It was during the 1850s that the development of South Dakota's agriculture began. Land promoters bought up land in 1857, establishing the towns of Sioux Falls, Medary, Yankton, Bon Homme, and Vermillion within a few years. In 1861 Congress created the Dakota Territory. But severe difficulties with the Indians, specially the Sioux, followed. The Sioux were forced to sign a treaty with the government giving land in southeastern South Dakota to the United States and restricting the tribe to reservations. Controversies over new roads and trespassing onto these Indian reservations soon ed to uprisings. When gold was discovered on the Sioux reservation n the Black Hills in 1874, thousands of settlers poured in. Many who came during the gold rush stayed on to farm, and the Sioux were finally forced to relinquish their land in 1877. In 1878 came "the great Dakota boom"—a land rush in which numerous farmers

U.S. cavalrymen bury Indians massacred in the 1890 Battle of Wounded Knee, in which some 200 Sioux warriors, women, and children were shot down at Wounded Knee Creek. This slaughter effectively ended Indian resistance and was the last major engagement between U.S. Army soldiers and Indians in American history.

and speculators entered the state. The population swelled from 12,000 in 1870 to 348,600 in 1890, when the Indian Wars effectively ended with the massacre of Indian families at Wounded Knee. By 1886 railroads had been built across South Dakota, and many towns blossomed along the right of way.

In 1889 Congress set the present boundary between North and South Dakota, the former Dakota Territory, and in November of that year South Dakota entered the Union as the 40th state. In the early 1900s, farm land was in demand and crop prices were high. A a result, thousands of settlers came to live in the state.

Then came the Great Depression of the 1930s. Not only were South Dakota farmers faced with decreased demand and prices for their products, they were also suffering through a terrible drought coupled with a grasshopper plague that began in 1930 and lasted fo 10 years.

The demand for agricultural products during World War II strengthened South Dakota's economy, and dams built by the Missouri River Basin Project created more jobs and power for the development of industry. Ben Reifel became the first Native Ameri can to represent South Dakota in Congress. In 1973, 200 Native Americans including members of the American Indian Movement (AIM) occupied the village of Wounded Knee to bring attention to the needs of Native Americans and to protest federal policies relat ing to Indians. The protest ended when Native Americans were assured that their grievances would be addressed. The occupation lasted over two months and resulted in 2 deaths and more than 300 arrests.

South Dakota has diversified its economy with the manufacture of clothing, machinery, metals, and other products. As farm exports declined in the 1980s, farm prices dropped, and interest rates increased. The average farmer's salary declined and many farmers were forced to sell their land when they could not pay their mortgages. To attract corporations to the state and to encour age young people to remain in the state, political leaders note that

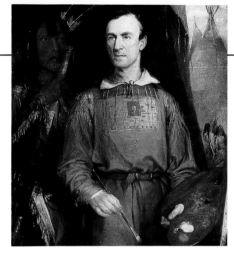

Far left:
Sitting Bull, one of the most renowned Indian leaders of all time, was born near Grand River in the 1830s. As chief of the northern Sioux, he won fame as a tribal warrior in the 1860s, together with Oglala Sioux leader Crazy Horse. During the 1870s they led the confederation of Sioux, Arapaho, and Cheyenne that overwhelmed General Custer and his men at the Battle of Little Bighorn.

Above right:
George Catlin, one of America's most famous painters of the Western Indians, spent much of his career in South Dakota and other areas on the Great Plains. He was captivated by life on the prairies and dedicated himself to learning the way of life of his Indian subjects.

Below:
Traditional Czech costumes are worn at one of South Dakota's ethnic festivals. The land boom of the late 1800s brought settlers from many European countries.

South Dakota does not tax personal or corporate incomes, and the state has notably clean air and water.

Education

The first schoolhouse in the South Dakota region opened in 1860 in Bon Homme, but it had to be torn down within three months so that its logs could be used to build a stockade for protection against the Indians. The territorial legislature authorized a public-school system in 1862, after the first institute of higher education, Augustana College, was founded in 1860.

The People

Approximately 29 percent of South Dakotans live in metropolitan areas. About 98 percent of them were born in the United States. Most of those born in other countries came from Denmark, Germany, Norway, Russia, and Sweden. The largest single religious group is the Lutheran. The second largest is the Roman Catholic Church, followed by the Methodists, Presbyterians, and members of the United Church of Christ.

Famous People

Many famous people were born in the state of South Dakota. Here are a few:

Sparky Anderson b. 1934, Bridgewater. Baseball manager

Floyd Bannister b. 1955, Pierre. Baseball pitcher

Tom Brokaw b. 1940, Webster. Television journalist

Dave Collins b. 1952, Rapid City. Baseball player

Hallie Flanagan 1890-1969, Redfield. Playwright

Joe Foss b. 1915, near Sioux Falls. Governor, military hero, and American Football League president

Gall 1840-94, on Moreau River. Indian leader

Philip L. Graham 1915-63, Terry. Journalist and publisher

John Grass 1837-1918, near Grand River. Indian leader

Edith Green 1910-87, Trent. Congresswoman

Alvin Hansen 1887-1975, Viborg. Economist

Mary Hart b. 1951, Sioux Falls. Television host: *Entertainment Tonight*

Hubert Humphrey 1911-78, Wallace. Vice-President and Senate leader

Cheryl Ladd b. 1951, Huron. Television and film actress: *Charlie's Angels*

Ernest O. Lawrence 1901-58, Canton. Nobel Prize-winning physicist

George McGovern b. 1922, Avon. Senate leader and presidential candidate

Earl Sande 1898-1968, Groton. Jockey

Carl L. Schmidt 1885-1946, Brown County. Biochemist

Sitting Bull 1834-90, on Grand River. Indian leader

Norm Van Brocklin 1926-83, Eagle Butte. Hall of Fame football quarterback

Colleges and Universities

There are many colleges and universities in South Dakota. Here are the more prominent, with their locations, dates of founding, and undergraduate enrollments.

Augustana College, Sioux Falls, 1860, 1,929

Black Hills State College, Spearfish, 1883, 2,814

Dakota State University, Madison, 1881, 1,504

Dakota Wesleyan University, Mitchell, 1885, 766

Huron University, Huron, 1883, 1,076

Mount Marty College, Yankton, 1922, 1,104

Northern State University, Aberdeen, 1901, 2,867

Sioux Falls College, Sioux Falls, 1883, 552

South Dakota School of Mines and Technology, Rapid City, 1885, 2,444

South Dakota State University, Brookings, 1881, 8,550

University of South Dakota, Vermillion, 1862, 7,591

Where To Get More Information

South Dakota Tourism
711 East Wells Ave.
Pierre, SD 57501-3369
or call, 1-800-SDAKOTA

Wyoming

The seal of the state of Wyoming, adopted in 1893, shows a woman standing on a pedestal holding a banner containing the state motto. Male figures on each side of the pedestal represent the mining and livestock industries. The dates 1869 and 1890, which appear below the pedestal, are the years that Wyoming became a territory and a state. "Great Seal of the State of Wyoming" is printed in the border.

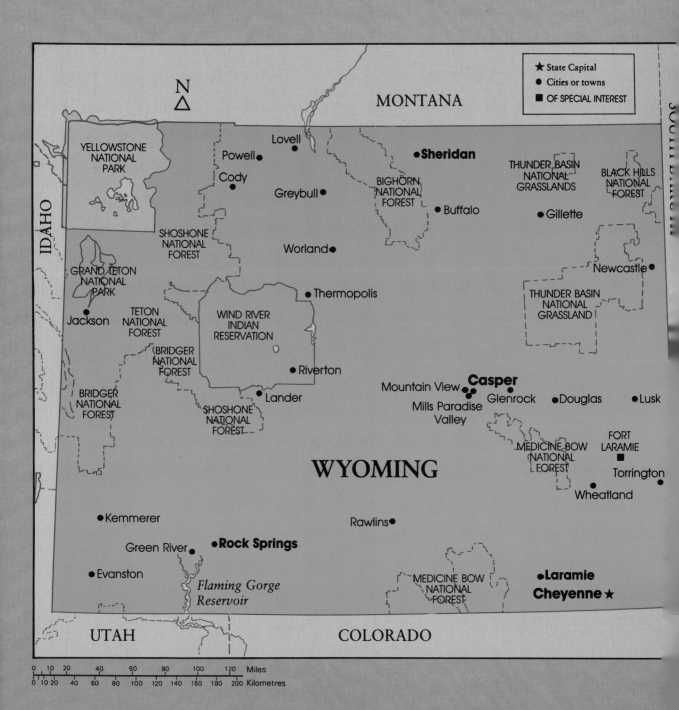

N
△

MONTANA

★ State Capital
● Cities or towns
■ OF SPECIAL INTEREST

IDAHO

YELLOWSTONE
NATIONAL
PARK

Lovell

Powell

Cody

Greybull

●Sheridan

BIGHORN
NATIONAL
FOREST

THUNDER BASIN
NATIONAL
GRASSLANDS

BLACK HILLS
NATIONAL
FOREST

● Buffalo

● Gillette

SHOSHONE
NATIONAL
FOREST

Worland●

GRAND TETON
NATIONAL
PARK

● Thermopolis

Newcastle●

THUNDER BASIN
NATIONAL
GRASSLAND

Jackson

TETON
NATIONAL
FOREST

WIND RIVER
INDIAN
RESERVATION

BRIDGER
NATIONAL
FOREST

BRIDGER
NATIONAL
FOREST

● Riverton

SHOSHONE
NATIONAL
FOREST

● Lander

Mountain View ●●**Casper**

Mills Paradise ●Glenrock
Valley

●Douglas

●Lusk

FORT
LARAMIE
■

MEDICINE BOW
NATIONAL
FOREST

WYOMING

● Torrington

Wheatland

●Kemmerer

Rawlins●

●Rock Springs

Green River●

●Evanston

Flaming Gorge
Reservoir

MEDICINE BOW
NATIONAL
FOREST

●**Laramie**

Cheyenne ★

UTAH

COLORADO

0 10 20   40   60   80   100   120   Miles
0 10 20   40   60   80   100 120 140 160 180 200 Kilometres

WYOMING
At a Glance

Capital: Cheyenne

Major Industries:
Minerals, tourism, agriculture, livestock
Major Crops: Wheat, beans, barley, oats
State Motto: Equal Rights
State Tree: Cottonwood
Nicknames: Cowboy State, Equality State
State Song: "Wyoming"

State Flag

State Bird: Meadowlark

Size: 97,809 square miles (9th largest)
Population: 466,185 (nation's smallest)

State Flag

The state flag of Wyoming, adopted in 1917, contains the state seal in the center of the white silhouette of a buffalo on a blue field. The flag is enclosed by a white inner border, which stands for purity, and a red outer border, which represents the blood of the pioneers and the Indians.

State Motto
Equal Rights

The state motto, officially adopted in 1955, refers to the fact that in 1869, Wyoming became the first state to give women the right to vote.

Winter lays claim to Yellowstone Park.

State Capital

Cheyenne became the territorial capital of Wyoming in 1869 and continued as state capital after Wyoming was admitted to the Union in 1890.

State Name and Nicknames

The name Wyoming comes from the Delaware Indian word *mecheweamiing*, which means "upon the great plain."

Wyoming is often called the *Equality State* because it was the first state to give women the right to vote. Other nicknames include the *Cowboy State, Big Wyoming,* and *Wonderful Wyoming.*

State Flower

Indian paintbrush, *Castilleja linariaefolia*, was chosen state flower in 1917.

State Tree

The plains cottonwood, *Populus sargentii*, was named state tree in 1947 and again in 1961.

State Bird

In 1927, the meadowlark, *Sturnella neglecta*, was selected state bird.

State Gemstone

Jade was designated state gemstone in 1967.

State Mammal

The American bison, *Bison americanus*, was adopted state mammal in 1985.

State Song

"Wyoming," with words by Charles E. Winter and music in two versions, one by George E. Knapp, and one by Earle R. Clemens, was named state song in 1955.

Population

The population of Wyoming in 1992 was 466,185, making it the least populated state in the nation. There are 4.64 people per square mile.

Industries

Mining is the most important industry in Wyoming. The production of uranium, coal, natural gas, petroleum, and other minerals comprises 26 percent of the goods and services produced in Wyoming every year.

The chief manufactured goods are refined petroleum products, foods, wood products, stone, clay, and glass products.

Agriculture

The chief crops of the state are wheat, beans, barley, oats, sugar beets, and hay. Wyoming is also a livestock state; there are estimated to be 1.3 million cattle, 24,000 hogs and pigs, and 850,000 sheep on its farms. Aspen and yellow pine are harvested. Portland cement and crushed stone are important mineral resources.

Government

The governor is elected to a four-year term, as are the secretary of state, auditor, treasurer, and superintendent of public instruction. The state legislature, which meets annually, consists of a 30-member Senate and a 62-member House of Representatives. Senators serve four-year terms, and representatives serve two-year terms.

In addition to its two United States senators, Wyoming has one representative in the U. S. House of Representatives. The state has three votes in the electoral college.

Sports

Many sporting events on the collegiate and secondary school levels are played throughout the state. In football, the University of Wyoming won the Gator Bowl in 1951, and the Sun Bowl in 1956, 1958, and 1966. The school also won the NCAA basketball championship in 1943.

Major Cities

Casper (population 46,765). Founded in 1888, Casper became an oil town when the first well was drilled in 1889.

The demand for oil during World War I brought prosperity to the town. Today, tourism, agriculture, and mining have joined oil as the city's major industries.

Things to see in Casper:
Fort Casper Museum, Natrona County Pioneer Museum, Nicolaysen Art Museum and Discovery Center, Werner Wildlife Museum, Edness K. Wilkins State Park, Casper Mountain and Beartrap Meadow Parks, Lee McCune Braille Trail, Alcova Lake Park, and Dan Speas Fish Hatchery.

Cheyenne (population 50,008). Founded in 1867 as a division point on the Union Pacific Railroad, Wyoming's largest city is also the state's capital. It was named for the Shahiyenan Indians of the Algonquin tribe. It quickly developed a reputation as Hell on Wheels because of the gunmen, gamblers, and confidence men who operated there. It is the retail and banking center of the region. Cattle and sheep ranching, coal, oil, and timber are important industries.

Things to see in Cheyenne:
State Capitol, Historic Governors' Mansion State Historic Site, State Museum and Art Gallery, Warren Air Force Base, National First Day Cover Museum, Cheyenne Frontier Days Old West Museum, Holiday Park, Wildlife Visitor Center, and Curt Gowdy State Park.

Laramie (population 26,687). Settled in 1868, the town was named after Jacques LaRamie, a French-Canadian trapper who occupied the region during the 1820s. The site was on the old Overland Trail and Pony Express route. Today, Laramie is a trading center for stock-raising, a mining region, and a manufacturing center, as well as a summer and winter resort area.

Things to see in Laramie:
Laramie Plains Museum, The Western Historical Collection in the University of Wyoming Library, Fine Arts Center, and the Geological Museum.

Places to Visit

The National Park Service maintains eight areas in the state of Wyoming: Yellowstone National Park, Grand Teton National Park, Devils Tower National Monument, Fossil Butte National Monument, Fort Laramie National Historic Site, Bighorn Canyon Recreation Area, Flaming Gorge Recreation Area, and Thunder Basin National Grassland. In addition, there are ten state recreation areas.

Built in 1834, Fort Laramie was the earliest permanent white settlement in Wyoming.

Alcova: Independence Rock State Historic Site. The names of more than 5,000 pioneers are carved into this 193-foot-high granite boulder.

Cody: Buffalo Bill Historical Center. The four museums that comprise the center detail the art, crafts, culture, and history of the American West.

Douglas: Wyoming Pioneer Memorial Museum. The museum features a large collection of pioneer and Indian artifacts from the 1800s. Fort Fetterman State Historic Site, a museum of the old officers' quarters.

Guernsey: Oregon Trail·Ruts National Historic Landmark, section of the Oregon Trail where wagon wheels left deep track marks in the soft sandstone above the North Platte River.

Jackson: Aerial Tramway. The two-and-a-half-mile ride carries visitors to the top of Rendezvous Mountain, 10,450 feet above sea level.

Medicine Bow: Como Bluff Fossil Cabin. The cabin, constructed entirely of dinosaur bones, features a museum containing rocks and artifacts of the area.

Riverton: Riverton Museum. This museum features Shoshone and Arapaho costumes, and demonstrations of pioneer skills, such as silversmithing and quilting.

Sheridan: Bradford Brinton Memorial-Museum and Historic Ranch. The 20-room main house contains works of art by American artists Charles M. Russell and Frederic Remington, among others.

South Pass City: This gold-mining boomtown was founded in 1867 and lasted until 1872. There are over 20 historic buildings to visit here.

Events

There are many events and organizations that schedule activities of various kinds in the state of Wyoming. Here are some of them.

Sports: Polo matches (Big Horn), Central Wyoming Fair Race Meet (Casper), Casper Classic Bicycle Races (Casper), Cody Stampede (Cody), Cody Nite Rodeo (Cody), Cowboy Days (Evanston), Para Ski Championships (Jackson), Jackson Hole Rodeo (Jackson), Old-Timer's Rodeo (Lander), One Shot Antelope Hunt (Lander), Pack Horse Race (Pinedale), Pen-to-Pen Run (Rawlins), Rocky Mountain All-Girl Rodeo (Rock Springs), Flaming Gorge Fishing Tournament (Rock Springs), Red Desert Round-up (Rock Springs), Saratoga Ice Fishing Derby (Saratoga), Sheridan-Wyo PRCA Rodeo (Sheridan), Silver Bullet Bike Race (Worland).

Arts and Crafts: Jackson Hole Fall Arts Festival (Jackson), Mountain Artist's Fest Rendezvous (Jackson), Saratoga Craft Fair (Saratoga).

Music: Grand Teton Music Festival (Jackson), Grand Targhee Music Festival (Jackson), State Championship Old-time Fiddle Contest (Riverton), Cowboy Music and Poetry Festival (Riverton).

Entertainment: Lincoln County Fair (Afton), Bozeman Trail Days (Buffalo), Buffalo Merchants Crazy Days (Buffalo), Christmas Parade (Buffalo), Central Wyoming Fair and Rodeo (Casper), Cottonwoods Festival (Casper), Cheyenne Frontier Days (Cheyenne), Western Plains Fair (Cheyenne), Buffalo Bill Birthday Celebration (Cody), Frontier Festival (Cody), Main Street Festival (Cody), Plains Indians Powwow (Cody), Jackalope Days (Douglas), Wyoming State Fair (Douglas), Winter Carnival (Dubois), Buffalo Barbeque (Dubois), Wind River Rendezvous (Dubois), Chili Cook-off (Evanston), Uinta County Fair (Evanston), Mountain Man Rendezvous (Evanston), Bridger Valley Pioneer Days (Fort Bridger), Fort Bridger Rendezvous (Fort Bridger), Flaming Gorge Days (Green River), Days of '49 Celebration (Greybull), Covered Wagon Cookout and Wild West Show (Jackson), Wyoming Winter Fair (Lander), Pioneer Days (Lander), Jubilee Days (Laramie), Elizabethan Fair (Laramie), Laramie River Rendezvous (Laramie), Mustang Days (Lovell), Medicine Bow Days (Medicine Bow), Whoop 'n Holler Days (Newcastle), Winter Carnival (Pinedale), Wyoming Wheels Weekend (Pinedale), Indian Powwows (Riverton), Sweetwater County Fair (Rock Springs), Sierra Madre Winter Carnival (Saratoga), Goshen County Fair (Torrington), Dad Worland Days (Worland), Washakie County Fair (Worland).

Tours: Wyoming River Trips (Cody), Wild West Jeep Tours (Jackson), Wagon Treks (Jackson), Fort Jackson Float Trips (Jackson).

Theater: Gertrude Krampert Summer Theatre (Casper), Atlas Theater (Cheyenne), Jackson Hole Playhouse (Jackson), Pink Garter Theater (Jackson), Dirty Jack's Wild West Theater and Opera House (Jackson), Green River Rendezvous (Pinedale), Legend of Rawhide Pageant (Lusk), Variety Theatre (South Pass City), Gift of the Waters Pageant (Thermopolis).

Yellowstone National Park has more geysers than any other site in the world.

Wyoming attracts visitors with its wide range of fascinating areas. Besides many historical frontier sites, the state offers an impressive array of distinctive natural wonders, from the rugged Black Hills to the soaring Teton Mountains to the spectacular geyser Old Faithful.

The Land and the Climate

Wyoming's terrain is both varied and dramatic, as a result of ancient volcanic action and erosion from rivers, streams, and mountain runoff. Floods and great surges of water through narrow channels have created deep gorges and canyons that are a breathtaking feature of the state's topography.

Wyoming contains much flatland suitable for cattle and sheep grazing.

Wyoming is bordered on the west by Idaho and Utah, on the north by Montana, on the east by South Dakota and Nebraska, and on the south by Utah and Colorado. The state has three major land areas: the Great Plains, the Rocky Mountains, and the Intermontane Basins

The Great Plains are located in a narrow strip along the eastern border, and are part of the huge interior plain of North America that extends from Canada to Mexico. Much of it is covered by short, tough grass that supports numerous cattle, sheep, and other livestock. The Black Hills are located in the northeastern part of this region and extend into South Dakota.

The Rocky Mountains sweep across the state in huge ranges. They include the Bighorn Mountains, the Laramie Range, the Granite Mountains, the Teton Ranges, and others. In the Wind River Range is the highest point in the state—13,785-foot Gannett Peak. There is some ranching and farming in the region, as well as coal mines and natural-gas and oil fields.

The Intermontane Basins consist of flat areas between the mountain ranges. Although rainfall is sparse here, the grasslands are ideal for raising cattle and sheep and irrigation has increased the land's productivity.

Parts of three great river systems begin in the mountains of Wyoming: the Missouri, the Colorado, and the Columbia systems. Many of their rivers have cut deep canyons, where spectacular waterfalls descend from high cliffs. Wyoming has hundreds of clear, cold mountain lakes.

Temperatures and weather conditions vary greatly with altitude, although generally Wyoming's climate is dry and sunny. In January, readings of 22 degrees Fahrenheit in central Wyoming and 12 degrees F. in northwestern Yellowstone National Park are not uncommon. July readings in these areas average 71 degrees F. and 5 degrees F., respectively. Snowfall is extremely high in the mountains

The History

There were probably Indian hunters in what was to become Wyoming more than 11,000 years ago, and when huge herds of buffalo began roaming the prairies, they lured many tribes into the area. When the first white men arrived in the region, they found the Arapaho, Bannock, Blackfoot, Cheyenne, Crow, Flathead, Nez Percé, Shoshone, Sioux, and Ute tribes.

The first Europeans to come into the Wyoming territory may have been the French-Canadian brothers François and Louis-Joseph de la Vérendrye, who arrived in 1743. But exploration of the area did not begin until after the United States bought the Louisiana Territory, which included Wyoming, from France in 1803. After that, American trappers came in search of furs and one of them, John Colter, explored the Yellowstone region in 1807.

In 1834 Fort Laramie, the area's first permanent trading post, was established. Others, such as Fort Bridger, sprang up as the demand for furs increased, and settlers moved in to work the land. During the 1820s and 1830s, the fur trade was the most important activity in the region.

By the 1850s, a steady stream of families in covered wagons was heading westward. But the Plains Indians, alarmed at this invasion of their land, began attacking wagon trains, leading to prolonged warfare between the Indians and the United States government.

Both skirmishes and pitched battles continued until 1868, when the Sioux were forced to sign a treaty at Fort Laramie by which they gave up most of their lands except for the northeastern part of the Wyoming Territory, which was created that same year. The Indians also agreed not to interfere with track-laying for the Union Pacific Railroad through southern Wyoming. Then gold was discovered in the Black Hills in 1874, and thousands of prospectors violated the treaty by moving into the Sioux reservation. The battles between the Sioux and the U.S. cavalry began again.

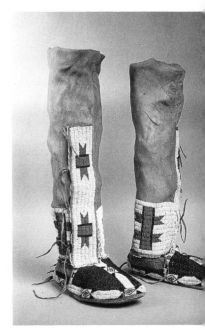

A pair of knee-high moccasins crafted by Shoshone Indians of Wyoming. The Shoshone were among the many Plains Indian tribes to settle in the region, which was prized for its large herds of buffalo and other game animals.

James Bridger, a trapper and guide, was one of the most colorful figures in early Wyoming history. In 1843 he completed Fort Bridger, a trading post along the Oregon Trail. The fort later became a U.S. military post.

Several towns had been established before 1870, both along the Union Pacific tracks and along the pioneer trails that crossed the state, notably the Oregon and the Mormon Trails. The cattle industry was well established. In 1869 the territorial legislature became the first to grant women the right to vote, hold office, and serve on juries.

Wyoming became the 44th state of the Union in 1890, which opened the door to a new influx of settlers. At this point, fresh troubles arose among owners of large cattle ranches who accused newcomers of stealing from their herds. Cattle rustling led to bloodshed, including the Johnson County Cattle War of 1892.

More settlers arrived as word spread about Wyoming's excellent grazing land. Homestead acts in 1909, 1912, and 1916 provided free land for development, and the discovery of oil at Salt Creek Field near Casper in 1912 gave the economy an additional boost. Irrigation of prairie lands increased the state's agricultural output. In 1924 Wyoming elected the nation's first woman governor, Nellie Tayloe Ross. Governor Ross was elected to succeed her husband, William B. Ross, after his death earlier that year.

Wyoming was not as hard hit by the Great Depression of the 1930s as other Western states. The economy was bolstered by oil production, and the federal government constructed dams and hydroelectric stations, including those of the Kendrick Project on the North Platte River. With the coming of World War II, the state began to boom: the nation needed its coal, lumber, meat, and oil. Shortly after the war, the discovery of uranium triggered new industrial development. In 1958 the F.E. Warren Air Force Base, the first U.S. intercontinental ballistic missile base, brought jobs and the defense industry to Wyoming. In the late 1960s and 1970s state leaders made a concentrated effort to attract manufacturing plants and industries to Wyoming to diversify the economy.

Today, Wyoming remains economically sound, with tourism as a major component of its prosperity. Millions of visitors come to Yellowstone, the nation's first national park, and enjoy the other natural wonders of the state.

"Buffalo Bill" Cody, Wild West showman and scout, founded what is now the town of Cody, Wyoming, around 1895. The town was originally a large ranch established with the aid of a land grant from the state.

Education

The first school in Wyoming was founded at Fort Laramie in 1852, and the first high school was opened at Cheyenne in 1868. Today, Wyoming's public schools are considered small and have very low teacher-student ratios. In many isolated areas of Wyoming, kindergarten to eighth-grade students attend one-teacher schools. The only accredited four-year university in the state is the University of Wyoming, which was established in 1887. It opened as a land-grant institution with a handful of students. Today it has numerous programs of study, including agriculture, the arts and sciences, commerce and industry, education, engineering, law, nursing, pharmacy, and it has a graduate school. In addition, Wyoming maintains two-year community colleges in Casper, Cheyenne, Powell, Riverton, Rock Springs, Sheridan, and Torrington.

The People

Approximately 30 percent of Wyomingites live in metropolitan areas and about 98 percent of them were born in the United States. Cheyenne, Laramie, and Casper are among the most populous urban areas. Wyomingites have come to the United States from countries as diverse as Scandinavia, China, Germany, Russia, Italy, Greece, and Ireland. Approximately 7,000 Native Americans live in Wyoming, and more than half, including Northern Arapahoe and Shoshone Indians, live on the Wind River Indian reservation. The largest religious groups in the state are the Baptists, Congregationalists, Episcopalians, Lutherans, Methodists, Mormons, Presbyterians, and Roman Catholics.

Wild-West rodeos are still among the most popular entertainment events in Wyoming.

Famous People

Many famous people were born in or relocated to the state of Wyoming. Here are a few:

Thurman W. Arnold 1891-1969, Laramie. U.S. assistant attorney general

Tom Browning b. 1960, Casper. Baseball pitcher

Martha Jane "Calamity Jane" Burk 1852?-1903, Missouri. Frontierswoman

Joseph Maull Carey 1845-1924, Delaware. Governor, U.S. attorney, and U.S. senator

Don Cockroft b. 1945, Cheyenne. Football player

William Frederick "Buffalo Bill" Cody 1846-1917, Iowa. Frontiersman and entertainer

Mike Devereaux b. 1963, Casper. Baseball player

Boyd Dowler b. 1937, Rock Springs. Football player

June Etta Downey 1884-1932, Laramie. Psychologist and author

Dick Ellsworth b. 1940, Lusk. Baseball pitcher

Francis Emroy 1844-1929, Massachusetts; Mayor of Cheyenne, last territorial governor and first state governor; U.S. senator

Curt Gowdy b. 1919, Green River. Broadcaster

Ferdinand Vandiveer Hayden 1829-1887, Massachusetts. Pioneer Rocky Mountain geologist

Grace Raymond Hebard 1861-1936, Iowa. Historian and feminist

Jerry Hill b. 1939, Torrington. Football player

Emerson Hough 1857-1923, Iowa. Author

John B. Kendrick 1857-1933, Texas. Governor and U.S. senator

Frank Wheeler Mondell 1860-1939, Missouri. Political leader

Edgar Wilson "Bill" Nye 1850-1896; Maine. Humorist

Jackson Pollock 1912-56, Cody. Artist

Nellie Tayloe Ross 1876-1977, Missouri. First woman governor in the U.S.

Alan K. Simpson b. 1931, Cody. Senate leader

Howard M. Snyder 1881-1970, Cheyenne. U.S. Army officer and physician

Spotted Tail 1833-81, near Fort Laramie. Indian leader

Willis Van Devanter 1859-1941, Indiana. Justice of U.S. Supreme Court

James Watt b. 1938, Lusk. U.S. Secretary of the Interior

Owen Wister 1860-1938, Pennsylvania. Novelist

Colleges and Universities

There is one four-year university in Wyoming; here is its location, date of founding, and undergraduate enrollment. In addition, there are several two-year colleges in the state.

University of Wyoming, Laramie, 1886, 12,052

Where To Get More Information

Travel Commission
Etchepare Circle
Cheyenne, WY 82002
or call, 1-800-CALLWYO

Further Reading

General

Grabowski, John F. and Patricia A. Grabowski. *State Reports: The Great Plains: Montana, Nebraska, North Dakota, South Dakota & Wyoming.* New York: Chelsea House, 1992.

Montana

Carpenter, Allan. *Montana,* rev. ed. Chicago: Childrens Press, 1979.

Fradin, Dennis B. and Judith Bloom Fradin. *From Sea to Shining Sea: Montana.* Chicago: Childrens Press, 1992.

Heinrichs, Ann. *America the Beautiful: Montana.* Chicago: Childrens Press, 1991.

Lang, William L. and Myers, R. C. *Montana: Our Land and People.* Boulder, CO: Pruett, 1979.

Nebraska

Carpenter, Allan. *Nebraska,* rev. ed. Chicago: Childrens Press, 1979.

Creigh, Dorothy Weyer. *Nebraska: A Bicentennial History.* New York: Norton, 1977.

Fradin, Dennis B. *Nebraska in Words and Pictures.* Chicago: Childrens Press, 1980.

Hargrove, Jim. *America the Beautiful: Nebraska.* Chicago: Childrens Press, 1988.

Nebraska: A Guide to the Cornhusker State. Lincoln, NE: University of Nebraska Press, 1979.

North Dakota

Carpenter, Allan. *North Dakota,* rev. ed. Chicago: Childrens Press, 1979.

Fradin, Dennis B. *North Dakota in Words and Pictures.* Chicago: Childrens Press, 1981.

Herguth, Margaret S. *America the Beautiful: North Dakota.* Chicago: Childrens Press, 1990.

Wilkins, Robert P. and Huchette, Wynona. *North Dakota: A Bicentennial History.* New York: Norton, 1977.

South Dakota

Carpenter, Allan. *South Dakota,* rev. ed. Chicago: Childrens Press, 1978.

Fradin, Dennis B. *South Dakota in Words and Pictures.* Chicago: Childrens Press, 1981.

Lepthien, Emilie U. *America the Beautiful: South Dakota.* Chicago: Childrens Press, 1991.

Milton, John R. *South Dakota: A Bicentennial History.* New York: Norton, 1977.

Wyoming

Bailey, Bernadine. *Picture Book of Wyoming,* rev. ed. Whitman, 1972.

Bragg, William F. *Wyoming: Rugged But Right.* Boulder, CO: Pruett, 1980.

Carpenter, Allan. *Wyoming,* rev. ed. Chicago: Childrens Press, 1979.

Fradin, Dennis B. and Judith Bloom Fradin. *From Sea to Shining Sea: Wyoming.* Chicago: Childrens Press, 1994.

Heinrichs, Ann. *America the Beautiful: Wyoming.* Chicago: Childrens Press, 1992.

Lamb, Russell. *Wyoming.* Portland: Graphic Arts Center, 1978.

Numbers in italics indicate illustrations

Picture Credits

Library of Congress: pp. 19 (left), 35, 73 (top), 74, 90; Courtesy of Montana Secretary of State: p. 5;
Museum of the American Indian: p. 89; National Portrait Gallery, Smithsonian Institution: pp. 19
(right), 20, 21 (right), 37 (top), 39 (bottom), 75 (top), 91 (top); Courtesy of Nebraska Department of
Economic Development: pp. 3 (bottom), 24, 26-27, 31, 32-33, 34, 36, 37 (bottom), 38, 39 (top);
Courtesy of Nebraska Secretary of State: p. 23; New York Public Library/Stokes Collection: p. 18
(bottom); Courtesy of North Dakota Secretary of State: p. 41; Courtesy of North Dakota Tourism
Promotion Division: pp. 4 (top), 43, 44-45, 47, 48, 49, 50, 51, 52, 53, 54-55, 56, 57, 58, 59; Courtesy of
South Dakota Office of Tourism: pp. 4 (middle), 62-63, 64-65, 66, 67, 68, 70, 71, 72, 73 (bottom), 75
(bottom); Courtesy of South Dakota Secretary of State: p. 61; Courtesy of Travel Montana
Department of Commerce: pp. 3 (top), 7, 12, 13, 14, 15, 16-17, 18 (top), 21 (left); Courtesy of Travel
Montana Department of Commerce/Steve Bly: pp. 8-9; Courtesy of Wyoming Division of Tourism:
pp. 4 (bottom), 79, 80-81, 84, 85, 86-87, 88, 92; Courtesy of Wyoming Secretary of State: p. 77.
Cover photos courtesy of Nebraska Department of Economic Development; North Dakota Tourism
Promotion Division; South Dakota Office of Tourism; Travel Montana Department of Commerce;
and Wyoming Division of Tourism.

40556